NEW WEAPONS
AND NATO

NEW WEAPONS
AND NATO

SOLUTIONS OR IRRITANTS?

Robert Kromer

CONTRIBUTIONS IN MILITARY STUDIES, NUMBER 66

Greenwood Press

NEW YORK · WESTPORT, CONNECTICUT · LONDON

Library of Congress Cataloging-in-Publication Data

Kromer, Robert Andrew, 1944–
  New weapons and NATO.

  (Contributions in military studies,
ISSN 0883-6884 ; no. 66)
  Bibliography: p.
  Includes index.
  1. North Atlantic Treaty Organization—Armed Forces.
2. North Atlantic Treaty Organization—Armed Forces—
Weapons systems.   3. Precision guided munitions.
4. Tactical nuclear weapons.   5. Strategic Defense
Initiative.   6. Europe—Military policy.   I. Title.
II. Series.
UA646.3.K76   1987   355'.031'091821   87-8649
ISBN 0-313-25588-1 (lib. bdg. : alk. paper)

British Library Cataloguing in Publication Data is available.

Library of Congress Catalog Card number: 87-8649
ISBN: 0-313-25588-1
ISSN: 0883-6884

First published in 1987

Greenwood Press, Inc.
88 Post Road West, Westport, Connecticut 06881

Printed in the United States of America

The paper used in this book complies with the
Permanent Paper Standard issued by the National
Information Standards Organization (Z39.48-1984).

10 9 8 7 6 5 4 3 2 1

Copyright Acknowledgment

The author and publisher gratefully acknowledge permission to reprint
material from the following copyrighted source.
James Digby. "Precision-Guided Munitions," *Adelphi Papers* 118. London:
International Institute for Strategic Studies, 1975.

Contents

Preface

This book is concerned with new weapon technologies and the North Atlantic Treaty Organization (NATO). I have chosen this particular topic because it combines two of my interests. As a professional military officer with over twenty years of service, I was charged with the responsibility of aiding my country to meet its security objectives. I took this charge most seriously. To meet those security objectives, I would have preferred to use the most modern, most effective means available. As a political scientist, however, I wanted the decisions to acquire and deploy certain weapons to be made with a full understanding of their actual and potential political effects upon this country and its allies. As this book will demonstrate, this has not always been the case. I prefer to study NATO because of its longstanding importance to the United States as a means of providing military security, because I want to understand better the nature of the disputes which constantly beset it, and because of past duty assignments with the alliance.

This book employs two case studies; they are in no way intended to represent the efforts of solely primary research. Much has been written of these two periods that is well documented and of high quality. While I will resort at times to primary materials, it will be my task to synthesize the secondary literature and to offer competing explanations for events as necessary.

Acknowledgments

This section of a book by tradition is reserved for some obligatory remarks about those individuals who have shown the author a particular kindness or have been constructively critical during the manuscript's journey to completion. In this particular case, I have more than enough reasons to give the usual "thanks." Successful completion of this book has required the circumvention of many obstacles (such as my normal job), long-distance coaching, and just plain tolerance by a number of people. Many persons have helped, some in small ways, others in larger measure. I am therefore particularly grateful to a variety of persons, but especially to Ole Holsti, who provided much critical advice during the manuscript's early form, and Colin Gray, who suggested several areas for consideration to make it more useful for a wider audience. Additionally, I would like to acknowledge the patience and support of LB&M Associates, who have provided me with a different perspective of the role of military analysts in the weapons acquisition process. When I first began this project, I was, perhaps, unduly critical of military analysts. Now that I am one, I am reminded of Walt Kelly's character "Pogo," who said, "I have met the enemy and he is us." In spite of all the assistance that I have identified, there remain weak areas in this book, for which I alone am responsible.

To
P.F.K.

NEW WEAPONS
AND NATO

1

The Lure of New Weapons

The American military always has a shopping list. It seeks planes that fly faster, submarines that dive deeper, or tanks that shoot straighter to replace its present weapons. It seems that last year's model is never good enough this year. If procured, these weapons are thought to increase markedly our military capabilities and thereby solve political problems. The North Atlantic Treaty Organization (NATO), as the premier American security alliance, has long been characterized as "in disarray," "crumbling," or worse. Some analysts think it would somehow be improved by adopting this or that new weapon; by their acquisition, new weapons would surely solve NATO's military problems and thereby increase NATO cohesion and unity. But there is much more to new weapons than their performance characteristics. The relationship of a weapon to its political environment may be more critical than its speed or lethality. This work examines the historical experiences of NATO with new weapon technologies and discerns their effect on the alliance. By understanding how NATO has been affected by new weapon technologies previously, perhaps the effect of future weapons can be assessed more accurately.

A REQUIREMENT FOR NEW WEAPONS

Nations go to war because there is nothing to prevent them from doing so. Kenneth Waltz's simple diagnosis is quite correct, if incomplete. Because of the nature of the international landscape, war has been a permanent feature of it. In recognition of the anarchic nature of the international political system, a nation-state, and particularly the domestic institution charged with providing its military security, seeks to obtain the most modern, the most effective means for prosecution of armed conflict. This inclination to possess modern weaponry is understandable. The paramount concern of any sovereign state is self-preservation, and the ethic of the profession arms requires that military forces be as prepared as possible to meet the state's security objectives.

Although many techniques have been tried to achieve a lasting harmony among nations, all have failed. The balancing of power via shifting coalitions of nations, enforced peace via the supremacy of a single state, collective security, peace through law, and disarmament efforts—all have failed to create permanent peace. The prudent state, while not seeking war, will prepare for it in a manner consistent with its political culture and economic constraints. The military institutions charged with providing that security can be expected, as part of their professional responsibility, to perform their functions effectively yet efficiently. Because the consequences of a failure to provide adequate security can be great, the military seeks to perform its tasks with the best possible resources available. It is this attribute of professionalism that drives the military to seek the most effective means or weapons systems to prosecute warfare.[1] However, this is only one facet of the weapons acquisitions rationale.

Stimuli for new weapon systems may also be generated by the environment of the state or by bureaucratic concerns. A state may react to an increased external threat which disturbs some predetermined ratio of military power between the two states. (For example, it was the policy of England during the nineteenth century to possess at least twice as many capital ships as any Continental power.) This may result in what has been called an "action-reaction" arms race if the first state feels threatened by the buildup by the other. Because lead times for development of modern systems are so long, often states must anticipate a hostile state's acquisition of new weaponry and act accordingly. This may further cloud the rationale for their acquisition. New weapon systems may also be sought for more parochial, political reasons. Writings employing explicit models of decision making, especially those dealing with Graham T. Allison's bureaucratic politics model, are replete with well-documented case studies involving the purchase of military hardware for which there is no mission,[2] which is unnecessary or redundant,[3] or which serves only as a payoff for previously contracted political debts.[4]

In addition to the variety of diffuse stimuli for weapons acquisition, there does not seem to be a careful consideration of the political aspects of the development of new weapons.[5] Most of the discussion and opposition concerning the development of tactical nuclear weapons, for example, occurred after they had been developed and deployed. The general reasons for this particular failure can only be speculated upon, but the secrecy inherent in the development of this new weapon precluded much "outside" discussion. Those individuals closest to the developmental process—individuals who were probably neither trained nor inclined to consider the political aspects of the case—were the only ones with the information to conduct such an analysis.[6] Thus the community most able to analyze critically the problem—academia—was generally excluded from the opportunity to do so.[7] In part as a reaction to that particular failure in assessing the full impact of a new weapon technology, the Departments of State and Defense developed additional agencies to coordinate military needs and foreign policy.[8] While such agencies have been successful in many of their efforts, the weapons acquisition process continues subject to a variety of political pressures and available evidence indicates that subservience to the national interest may not always be one of its hallmarks.[9]

THE PROBLEM

Especially within the military, there is a great tendency to seek new weaponry that offers greater capabilities and/or requires less expenditure of resources. Weapons with improved performance are constantly being sought by and offered to the military. Arguments for their acceptance and development usually focus on their performance characteristics. Because they possess some "better" capability, new weapons are seemingly automatic candidates for acquisition. However, it is not the performance characteristics, but the political implications of new weapon technology that are most critical if these weapons are to have the desired political effects. This is especially true in an era of great concern about "low intensity conflict" being waged for limited political objectives.

The problem of matching weapon system implications with desired political objectives is particularly acute for NATO. Recently, there has been much discussion of "flexible options" and "management of the level of conflict," reinforcing the notion that weapons are expected to perform political as well as military functions. There has been a marked tendency, especially among military analysts, to believe that if NATO could somehow become more efficient with what it has, or, even better, if it could acquire weapon "X," its military problems would be substantially solved and its political problems of cohesion and efficacy would be greatly reduced, if not resolved.[10] But NATO is a diplomatic instrument created to serve political goals. To this author, its cohesion and efficacy are therefore largely a function of the politics of the alliance, rather than the effect of any particular hardware. Because of this widespread misperception of the actual effects of weapon technology, analysis of this type is crucial. It is this author's intention to examine the consequences of the introduction of new weapon technology into NATO. By analyzing how NATO has reacted to new technologies in the past, this study will determine critical variables and relationships, and will use that information in making judgments about the effects of the introduction of new technologies into NATO in the future.

NEW TECHNOLOGIES—A NEED FOR STUDY

The study of the effects of technology is certainly not novel. There are many standard works on the results of innovations in technology, but these deal with non-military technology, or only in a general way with its effect on society.[11] The field of *military* technology is not without its specialists. It is replete with examinations of the effects of innovations on warfare and its implements. Until fairly recently, most of these detailed studies dealt with either the technology's effects upon the military (changes in tactics, or the doctrine of employment),[12] or only in a limited sense, upon society (the outcome of battles and wars,[13] or the relations between civil and military authorities[14]). In most cases these works do not go beyond a fairly narrowly defined description of the effect of the innovation, ignoring the larger political implications of the advancements, and the effect of the advancements upon the relations of nations. During the 1950s, many nonmilitary authorities formulated strategic doctrines for nuclear weapons employment, but most of that writing concerned a single new technology (nuclear weapons) and did not develop a generalized framework for the study of the effects of new weapon technology.[15]

Other attempts to deal with the problem of technology in NATO have pointed to the need for standardization of weaponry in NATO.[16] Here, various schemes for the production of either specific weapon systems or for classes of weapons by different members of NATO are propounded to enhance the effectiveness of the alliance, reduce spare parts loads, benefit the domestic economic situation, or enhance cohesion of the alliance. In these cases, the advent of a new weapon technology is taken as a "given." No analysis is made of the potential political effects of that technology upon the alliance.

But this is not to say that no thought has been given to the subject of how military innovations might affect the international political system and the behavior of states within it. Quincy Wright, in his monumental work on war, ascribed to military technology an "overwhelming" power, "obliging" states "to move in the direction of totalitarianism and to equip themselves with the latest devices, or place themselves under the protection of those states so equipped."[17] J. F. C. Fuller has seen in the inventiveness of man a "Frankensteinian monster . . . that is destroying man's own work, his own culture, his own civilization, his past, his present, his future."[18] Other texts describe the contribution of new technology to the breakdown of the "bipolar" world of the 1950s and the emergence of a "multipolar" world of the 1970s.[19] Other authors have described how these new technologies have created a web of interdependence among states and other transnational actors, thereby proscribing the nature and scope of their interactions in the international political system.[20]

These efforts in the area of military technology are quite useful as analyses of the modification of the relations among states but they still do not get at one of the more fundamental aspects of the analysis of new technology. In all of the works cited above, one may infer the assumption that the march of technology is inevitable and cannot be controlled; like Stowe's "Topsy," it will "just grow." Whether this assumption is valid is not the point here. Rather, the point is that new military technology must be more closely examined for its longer range impact on political events. "Muddling through" is simply not enough. Aside from the natural disposition of rational man to seek to control the outcome of events, there are more fundamental reasons why new military technology's effects should be examined in more detail.

Recent analyses of the problems of arms control have yielded valuable information about the likelihood for concluding arms control agreements. In examining the apparent preconditions for reaching arms control agreements, these studies have shown that the likelihood for success in reaching agreement on the control of a particular weapon system is enhanced if the weapon is in the early or terminal stage of its useful life.[21] If the weapon system is not operational, or if it is in a period of declining effectiveness, then the opportunity for limiting that system is increased over that of limiting a weapon system that is in its operational "prime." For example, the United States and the Soviet Union were able to conclude an agreement in 1972 limiting the deployment of antiballistic missile systems in part because neither side had a fully operational system at that time. The United States was in the process of research and development of its antimissile system and the Soviet Union then had only a low quality, unsophisticated system in operation. As an additional example, in 1974, the United States and the Soviet Union were able to conclude an agreement limiting the yield of nuclear weapons to be tested because both had developed sufficiently accurate missiles to allow the yields of the warhead of proposed missile systems to be below the maximum size permitted by the treaty. Hence, larger yield weapons were no longer required in order to produce the desired degree of effect on the target, so it was agreeable to prohibit testing of those higher yields. Testing of the newer, smaller yield weapons was left unaffected by this treaty.

The implications for the study of new military technology are clear. In order to enhance the probability of regulation of arms, efforts to do so should be conducted before those arms enter the production stage, for at that point, extraordinarily strong bureaucratic pressures for the maintenance of those weapons in the inventory are generated. Similarly, a study of the possible results of deploying new technology should include an examination of its effects upon one's allies. As indicated previously, little of a theoretical nature has been written on this subject thus far.

The high cost of new technology would also seem to require its examination. Always there exists within government a conflict over the use of scarce tax dollars. Of late, soaring deficits, bouyed by large defense budgets, threaten the fiscal solvency of the American government, and, ultimately, the world economy. Needlessly large defense expenditures preclude spending those monies on other programs. Of concern also is the suspicion that new or more weapons may not produce more security, but may actually reduce the level of security enjoyed by a state. For example, one must be certain that the trade-off between the achievement of enhanced military effectiveness through acquisition of a proposed new weapon is worth the possible increase in a potential opponent's apprehension that the weapon would be used against him. Perhaps more familiar is the debate as to whether acquisition of new military technology would be "destabilizing" and "refuel the arms race" in a type of action-reaction cycle, thereby necessitating the further expenditure of funds as the opponent seeks to counter your weapon system.[22]

If war is "too important to be left to the generals," then the preparation for war must also be important. The increased destructiveness of today's weapons, particularly nuclear weapons, requires examination of the political effects of their development. Political effects may vary in nature. Because of their awesome explosive power, it may be that the employment of these new weapons should be subject to special controls and authorizations, as is the case for all types of nuclear weapons belonging to the United States. Alternately, the distinctive signature of the explosion of a nuclear weapon may well be a signal that heretofore observed political and military limits on the conduct of the war have been exceeded, resulting in an escalation of the intensity of that war. In this case, limitations placed on military operations for the purpose of achieving political goals will have been exceeded, thereby hindering achievement of those goals. Although the special significance of the "firebreak" theory of nuclear weapons employment has been examined in some detail, it is precisely this kind of effort that must be expended for all types of military hardware, and in particular for new military technology.

TERMS AND SCOPE

Most new military hardware is usually only a modification of existing hardware. A new airplane may fly faster, carry more bombs, or have more electronic countermeasure equipment on board; a new rifle may have a faster rate of fire, a greater maximum effective range, or be lighter than its predecessors. The essential characteristics of these weapons, however, remain unchanged from the previous models and, as such, the political ramifications inherent in their development and employment might be expected to be relatively unchanged. New military technology is another case, however.

The term "new military technology" is used here to refer to technology that is so fundamentally different from the existing body of technology that present patterns of employment or measures of control must be changed. Technology is usually thought of as allowing scientific progress, and indeed it does. The microscope allowed for discovery and detailed examination of microorganisms and aided in the development of countless antibiotics for the treatment of diseases. In the relation between the two, increasingly in the past fifty years, scientific progress has exercised a strong influence on technology and it is precisely this relationship which will form the basis for our definition of new technology. In its broadest sense, technology may be defined as human activity whose object is to collect, adapt, or transform materials in order to affect conditions of human existence. Military technology would of course relate to the creation of such objects for application to warfare. For our purposes, military technology will be defined as the application of scientific or engineering knowledge to the production of weapons. Designation of what constitutes "new" technology is somewhat more difficult. As indicated, providing improvements to various operational weapon systems is quite routine and for many defense contractors constitutes the largest share of their production output, exceeding even the production of new weapons. But "new technology" is quite different from "modification" or "upgrade" of weapon systems.

Rather than being a routine modernization, the "new" of new technology indicates an innovative, novel, or unique occurrence. Because of a quantum change in accuracy, explosive power, or delivery technique, new military technology portends a radical departure from the established doctrine of the conduct, structure, and/or strategy of military operations. Brought about largely by the application of science to the production of war's weapons, new military technology will have a changed effect on its user and its intended target. In part, that effect will be purely military in nature. More or less men and equipment will be required. More or less user training with the new technology may be necessary. These items all carry a price tag of some sort and thus all require some political scrutiny. But these are not effects of the new technology that have the greatest potential for political effect.

While the questions of military effect are important, they are not the primary focus of this study. It is of greater significance to examine the broader questions of the effects of this new technology as it affects the military as an instrument of a nation's foreign policy. In order to limit the research question to one of more manageable proportions, and, as previously indicated, to correspond to the academic and military interests of the author, this work will deal with only a portion of those political effects—the effect of new weapon technology on NATO.

PROBLEM AREAS

In using the NATO alliance as the context for this study, it is recognized that certain "costs" are incurred. One of those costs relates to the "age" of the alliance. Because NATO has been in existence for a period of less than forty years, it may be difficult to sort out the specific effects of new technologies. Sufficient time may not have elapsed for the changes, or lack thereof, wrought by the new technology to percolate throughout the alliance and be discernible as such. This is certainly a possibility as regards the impact of the latest technology. It appears, however, that this will not be an insurmountable problem. By concentrating on the fundamental aspects of the alliance and its environment, the longer term trends may be assessed with greater confidence. Where caution is warranted, it will be exercised.

The use of the NATO alliance as the sole basis for study limits the degree of universality of the findings. If other alliances in other periods were examined also, any findings would enjoy wider applicability. However, the scope of this study has been limited intentionally. NATO has been a fixture of American foreign policy for almost four decades. If observations can be made which will benefit only the NATO alliance, that will be sufficient.

The term "NATO alliance" has been used thus far as if the alliance were a unified entity. Clearly, this is not the case. It is recognized fully that member nations of NATO have not compromised their respective sovereign rights by their membership in NATO.[23] NATO is not, of itself, a supranational organization, and its corporate decisions are not binding upon its members. Decisions made by its governing bodies must therefore be unanimous, or no decision is reached. Proposals encountering disagreement are either "watered down," made a part of some compromise, or discarded. Such are the requirements of sovereign states.

Militarily, NATO is not an organization which exercises command over forces. No forces nominally assigned to NATO are under the operational command of NATO—that is, under NATO's complete control. All member nations retain a "string" on their forces; they may recall or redirect their forces as they see fit. Operational orders to the various units must also be transmitted through national command channels. The several nation-members retain the final decision-making power, including command authority over forces "assigned" to NATO. Since not all members act and react alike, it may be presumptuous to talk about the technology and its impact on "NATO." However, for stylistic reasons, the term "NATO" will be used as a unitary actor. When appropriate, individual nations will be addressed and an attempt made to discern the total "NATO" implications.

METHODOLOGY

In performing historical research of this type, the statistical-correlation approach to the effects of weapon technology might well be employed. However, two problems immediately become obvious. First, the number of cases involving the incidence of new weapon technology in the NATO alliance is relatively small. Even if sufficient instances of emerging military technology could be selected, because of the short "life" of the alliance, the effects of those instances on the alliance would be difficult to discern. Secondly, combining elements of various cases into discreet categories in order to analyze statistically those cases in part robs those cases of their individual identity and obscures the more subtle nuances inherent in each case. These intervening variables may tend to alter from case to case in complex ways which cannot readily be compressed into a small number of meaningful, predefined categories for coding.

One may conclude, then, that the statistical-correlation approach needs to be supplemented with relatively intense analyses of individual cases, embracing a variety of variables. As indicated previously, intensive case studies of the effects of new military technology have been done. However, they have not been comparable; hence, their findings do not cumulate and prove little more than suggestive for any type of theory building or policy relevance. Not only have these previous case studies varied rather widely in their scope and intensity, they employ no systematic pattern for the conduct of research. The resultant loss of rigor does not augur well for other than a descriptive study of past phenomena.

The individual case study method possesses a set of virtues and deficiencies opposite to those of the statistical-correlation approach. Because each incident is studied individually, factors peculiar to that situation which may have been previously obscured by the statistical-correlation approach may be identified and causal links established. However, what is gained in richness and diversity is lost in scientific cumulativeness.

What is required, then, is a research methodology which is capable of identifying the diverse variables in one set of circumstances surrounding the initiation of new military technology from another set, while remaining cumulative across a series of cases. Happily, during the previous decade a more appropriate method was developed and applied by several analysts. Borrowing Alexander L. George and Richard Smoke's term, the method of *focused comparison* may be employed to extract the best of several research approaches.[24] By employing the same variables to explain multiple case studies, yet accounting explicitly for the variation of these factors from case to case, a focused comparison of the effects of new military technology will yield both richness and cumulativeness.

The approach to be used in this study of the effects of new military technology on the NATO alliance involves the use of a set of closely related questions/propositions concerning the alliance, the technology, and the international environment. Like the statistical-correlation approach, more than one case is studied using the same variables. But the focused comparison method also resembles the case study approach by permitting a more intense study of each case. Clearly, only a small number of cases can be studied using this method. In this study of NATO, only two instances of new military technology will be studied. However, by using a standardized framework for analysis, comparability of the results is enhanced.

To be sure, the method of a focused comparison has limitations. Employing only a small number of cases precludes the use of any statistical measure of association between independent and dependent variables. The findings must therefore be viewed with a lesser measure of confidence in their correctness. However, in place of a high degree of confidence offered by the large number of cases normally examined in the statistical-correlation approach, the focused comparison method has the advantage of policy relevance. By being able to select purposefully the individual cases to be studied, the researcher ensures that the specific variables that are of greatest importance to him are laid bare. Variables do not need to be selected because of their ease of measurement; the study is more efficient because only that which is of interest to the researcher is studied.

ALLIANCE THEORY AS A GUIDE TO RESEARCH

As indicated in the previous section underscoring the need for the study of new weapon technologies, the amount of literature on new technologies is sparse. Lacking this conceptual guidance, this author conducted a selective review of the traditional theoretical literature on alliances, which aided in focusing this research. The study of alliances is rich indeed, as one would expect from such a permanent fixture of statecraft. While works on international integration and regionalism abound within the overall topic of alliances, this study narrowed its focus to the theoretical works dealing with alliance behavior and, specifically, alliance unity and disintegration. Even within this refined subset, the literature was abundant but somewhat contradictory. To compound our difficulties, despite the plethora of theoretical literature on alliances, little of it dealt with technology. While thus making our research more difficult, it also becomes more necessary. As a neglected topic, new weapon technologies and alliance functioning offer an opportunity for important and relatively unique research.

That the literature is relatively silent on the role of technology within alliances is understandable, to a degree. Prior to the Industrial Revolution, revolutionary changes in technology in general and weapon technology in particular were few and far between. As an example, although the use of the longbow by English archers at Crécy in 1346 brought victory in that battle and a revision in the armaments and tactics of warfare, it had only a slight effect on existing alliances. Changes in military power among the combatants wrought by technology may have resulted in new calculations of relative alliance power, but technological changes, because they were slow in coming, were able to be absorbed by the alliances with relatively little effect within the alliance.

The rate of change of weapon technology has obviously increased over that of the Middle Ages. The powerful forces of the Industrial Revolution, when linked to the discoveries of science, have been primary factors causing this increased rate of change.

In the hundred years prior to the end of World War II, the repeating rifle, the oil-dampened recoil system for cannons, the machine gun, the tank, radar, sonar, and nuclear weapons were but a few of the revolutionary developments in weapons technologies during that period. These developments brought about revisions in the manner in which wars were fought, strategies to cause them not to be fought, and greater destructiveness when they were fought.

These changes in war's weapons continue at a rapid pace today, yet the literature on their effect on anything but the conduct of war is relatively scarce. While military analysts may write of changes in tactics, and systems analysts may calculate more exact measures of effectiveness, only sparse attention has been paid to the effects of new weapon technologies on alliances. This relatively neglected status of the theoretical literature, coupled with the rapid changes occurring in the development of today's weapons, is a major factor which points to the need for research in this important area.

This study will initially approach the topic of new weapon technologies and alliances via the concept of alliance behavior, and specifically, alliance cohesion, in an effort to illuminate critical variables and relationships.[25] To gain a sense of these factors, this author turned to the traditional literature on alliances in order to develop a preliminary framework for analysis of the effects of new weapon technologies on alliances.

In the preliminary research on the case studies, and from the initial approach to the topic of alliance behavior and cohesion, certain trends were clear. Some factors (such as the status of the environment of the alliance, the structure of the alliance, and the performance of the alliance) occurred repeatedly, indicating their importance for our consideration. Unhappily, this implied agreement of the importance of the factors did not produce agreement on either the nature of their behavior or the extent of their influence on alliances.

Aware of these conflicting conditions and with this general grouping of variables in mind, this author then turned to a survey of articles and books on international alliances with a view toward uncovering the major traditional explanations of alliance behavior.[26] While not exhaustive, this survey uncovered 347 separate propositions that deal with alliance behavior.[27] In reviewing these

propositions, many were determined to be relevant to our research because they could be classified into one of the three groups
described above, or they obviously dealt with new weapon technologies. Based on those initially identified propositions, this author conducted preliminary research into two case studies to determine the relevance of the propositions to the case studies. Based
on this initial "cut" of the case studies, the author then developed
the framework for analysis shown at Figure 1. The framework is
divided into six general subjects about which a series of research
questions have been developed.

THE RESEARCH FRAMEWORK

Since we are interested in the changes wrought by new weapon
technologies, it is necessary to divide the study into two temporal
parts—pre-technology and post-technology. The pre-technology
phase will allow us to establish referents by which change occurring in the post-technology phase may be detected. The first three
areas of the framework will establish those referents. The last three
areas will deal with the alliance in the era of the new technology
and will allow us to determine the nature and extent of the changes
to the alliance.

Pre-Technology—The International Political System. The review of
the survey on propositions of alliance behavior indicated that the
environment of the alliance is linked to the activities of its members.[28] Hence, the first section will deal with the international political system. Specifically, what was the nature and distribution
of power within the international political system? What was its
structure? Was it stable? What were the military, political, and
economic interactions of the states within the system?

Pre-Technology—The Alliance. Although relationships may indeed exist between the environment and the alliance, there are
aspects of the alliance itself which will affect its cohesion and efficacy and must therefore be a part of this framework for analysis.
Two general aspects of alliances which have received attention in
the alliance literature and relate to our study are the attributes of
alliance members and the attributes of the alliance itself.[29] What
was the relative distribution of political power within the alliance?

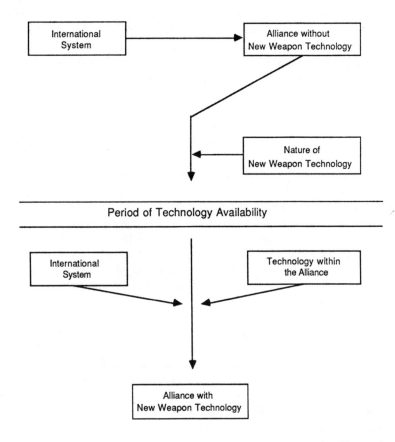

Figure 1
Schematic Diagram of Framework on New Weapon Technologies.

How did that distribution affect alliance cohesion? Did any member possess a "strategic culture" which affected its acceptance of alliance strategy—that is, were individual members predisposed toward certain concepts for organization of their resources and strategies for war? Did the differing concepts affect alliance cohesion and efficacy? What was the structure of the alliance? Was it relatively stable in size and structure? What were the governing structures of the alliance? What was the military strategy of the alliance? Was there general agreement on this strategy? Was the alliance supported in terms of resources such as personnel, equipment, and monetary support?

Pre-Technology—The Nature of the Technology. Having provided the basis for judging the status of NATO in the pre-technology era, the path is clear for an examination of the technology itself. What was the nature of the new technology? What were its general military characteristics? Was it affordable in economic or social terms by alliance members? Did it require special controls to regulate its employment? Was it compatible with existing alliance strategy?

The discussions of the international system and the alliance have centered on the pre-technology phase; the post-technology phase remains. As before, there are three areas of concern, but their content will vary somewhat from those of the preceding discussion. The first area, the international political system, or the environment, and its effect on the alliance, continues as a matter for investigation. In the second area, the alliance, the discussion will center on the status of the technology within the alliance. The net effect of these two dynamics will be the substance of the ultimate purpose of this study and the third area, the effect of the new weapon technology on NATO.

Post-Technology—The International Political System. From the preceding discussion on the international system, its structure, stability, and distribution of power were identified as key elements. How did the appearance of the new weapon technology affect those same aspects of the system? How did any such changes affect NATO cohesion and efficacy? What was the reaction of NATO's opponent, the Soviet Union/Warsaw Pact, to the new technology? Did the presence in the international political system of the new technology change the threat to the alliance or the system's structure and thereby affect alliance cohesion?

Post-Technology—The Technology within the Alliance. The second major area for examination in the post-technology era is the role of technology in the alliance. To what degree was the technology accepted/distributed within the alliance, as indicated by its density within the forces of alliance members and by the degree of agreement among alliance members on the strategy for its use? Did the possession of this technology change the distribution of political power within the alliance? Did the existence of the new technology cause a change to the governing structure of the alliance, and with what result in its performance? Did the new technology affect the existing strategy of the alliance and consequently the members' agreement on their tactical and strategic priorities?

Post-Technology—The Effect of the New Technology. The final portion of the framework is a net assessment of the results of the study of the previous two areas. This section will deal with the cumulative effect of the interaction of all the variables previously identified in the framework. It seeks to discern the overall effect of new weapon technology on the cohesion and efficacy of the alliance.

SELECTION OF CASES FOR STUDY

The case studies selected for examination in this study have met certain criteria. As previously noted, the NATO alliance has existed for almost forty years. During that time, many changes have occurred both within the alliance and to its environment. However, the incidence of new military technology, according to the definition previously offered, has not been as rapidly paced. A radical departure from a weapon's normal explosive power, accuracy, or delivery technique does not occur very often; hence, opportunities for cases to study within the life of the alliance are somewhat limited. However, a small number of opportunities for selection does not necessarily make for a limited quality of cases. In the past, some rather unique developments in the field of military technology would seem to qualify two different periods for inclusion in our study.

The six years of World War II saw many advances in military hardware, but by far the most significant military and political development was the atomic bomb. Generally regarded as the instrument which symbolized the Allies' power and the futility of continuance of the conflict by the Japanese, detonation of two atomic bombs against the Japanese brought an end to the war. Although it enhanced the military might of the West, it did not necessarily enhance its political influence, and relations worsened in what was to become a Cold War against the Soviet-dominated East.

To protect itself against a perceived Soviet-led threat from the East, nations of North America and Western Europe formed the North Atlantic Treaty Organization in 1949. As a peacetime military alliance, however, member nations were concerned about economic and social priorities as well as ensuring their military capability. For some members, then, the development of small yield atomic weapons which could be used on the tactical battlefield promised a partial solution to the dilemma of allocation of scarce resources. The technology that had been strategically decisive in World War II was to be applied to NATO's problem of containing the Soviets. Tactical nuclear weapons, as these devices became known, seemed to hold promise for a reduction of NATO military manpower and an increase in its firepower. What actually did transpire, however, was the development of greater disunity within the alliance, which makes this case fit for inclusion in our study. The case of tactical nuclear weapons for the alliance will be the first case studied.

The second period of the incidence of new technology to be studied is more recent. In the late 1960s, thanks mainly to scientific initiatives in the aerospace industries, microminiaturization of electronic circuitry enabled weapons to be fitted with on-board active guidance systems. This capability for in-flight correction of a weapon's trajectory greatly increased its accuracy. Precision-guided munitions, as these new weapons became known, seemed to promise to make "every shot a hit, and a hit became a kill." Relatively inexpensive, precision-guided munitions were proclaimed to be able to provide NATO with the superior firepower which would enable it to defeat the vastly numerically superior Warsaw Pact Treaty Organization. The real effect of these new weapons, however, was not their military firepower but was their political costs, if adopted. These political spillover effects, then, are what caused precision-guided munitions to be included as the other case study.

Before continuing with an examination of the two cases mentioned, it is appropriate to add a note about the manner in which the case studies will be approached. The author will examine each case individually, focusing on the research questions, and allowing each case to stand on its own merits. However, since the subject in both cases is the Atlantic Alliance, some carryover of factual information to the succeeding case will be presumed. Because this study will answer a series of questions about each case rather than provide a historical narrative, the chronological flow of events will be interrupted as necessary in order to digress for explanatory purposes. This author is content to do so since the purpose of this study is analytical rather than descriptive.

Structurally, this study will first examine the new era of tactical nuclear weapons and how the NATO alliance responded thereto. Next, precision-guided munitions and their impact will be examined. After explicating the results of the two studies and analyzing the findings in the final chapters, this author will draw conclusions about new military technology and check them against another new technology—the neutron bomb. Lastly, I will apply the conclusions to the latest controversy which promises to be the defense issue of the decade, the Strategic Defense Initiative, and offer some observations about how to reduce future turmoil in the alliance.

NOTES

1. There is a real danger in the development of "professionalism" in the military. The military, especially in America, has become deeply involved in the political process. The increasing technological sophistication of today's weapons creates military "experts," which, in turn, confers resources, corporate interests, and objectives to pursue. There is no guarantee that those interests and objectives are in consonance with the wants and needs of the public or even of the political elite. As a pressure group striving to claim scarce resources, the military will often strive to implement values and fulfill objectives that it defines to be central to its orga-

nizational essence. This view is in contradiction to Samuel P. Hunting-ton's thesis that political influence by the military can be eliminated through ensuring "professionalism." Huntington defines away the problem by stating "true professionals subscribe to civilian control." If one does not subscribe, one is not a professional. Therefore, to ensure civilian control, increase professionalism. For a fuller treatment of the concept of military professionalism and its relation to the political process, see Bengt Abra-hamson, *Military Professionalization and Political Power* (Beverly Hills, CA: Sage Publications, 1972), and Samuel P. Huntington, *The Soldier and the State* (Cambridge: Harvard University Press, 1957).

2. Graham T. Allison and Frederick T. Morris, "Armaments and Arms Control: Exploring the Determinants of Military Weapons," in *Arms, Defense Policy and Arms Control*, ed. Franklin A. Long and George W. Rathjens (New York: W.W. Norton and Company, 1976), p. 99.

3. Graham T. Allison and Richard Huff, "MIRV," in *Report of the Commission on the Organization of the Government for the Conduct of Foreign Policy*, vol. 4, appendix K: *Adequacy of Current Organization: Defense and Arms Control*, by Robert D. Murphy, Chairman (Washington, DC: U.S. Government Printing Office, 1975), p. 150.

4. John Steinbruner and Barry Carter, "Organizational and Political Dimensions of the Strategic Posture: The Problems of Reform," in Long and Rathjens, *Arms, Defense Policy and Arms Control*, p. 131.

5. The U.S. government's Arms Control and Disarmament Agency has long been required to submit "Impact Statements" for each item of nuclear hardware being considered for adoption by the military. The pur-pose of the Impact Statement is to assess the consequences for ongoing and future arms control actions as a result of adoption of the new hard-ware. This author is unable to recall a single instance where the agency cited proposed new hardware as being inimical to arms control efforts. The political effects of adoption of non-nuclear military hardware are even more rarely debated.

6. Ward Just asserts that the failure of American military officers to provide an intellectual contribution to the development of strategic thought is because an individual "Army officer has no time to think, and imagi-native reflection is discouraged. . . . The emphasis is on procedure, de-tail, fact, nut and bolt." *Military Men* (New York: Alfred A. Knopf, 1970), pp. 108-9.

7. In the 1950s, the interest of academia in military matters increased. Samuel P. Huntington makes this point quite clearly, stating that it was the limited perspectives of the military services that finally caused Amer-ican civilian strategists to get involved in the development of American strategic thinking. In so doing, the civilian strategists captured the field.

"After World War II, no book on strategy produced by an American military officer reached the sophisticated level of analysis of the best books on strategy by American civilians." Samuel P. Huntington, ed., *Changing Patterns of Military Politics* (New York: Free Press of Glencoe, 1962), p. 239. Also, it was in the early 1950s that the United States Air Force fostered the creation of a civilian "think tank" called The Rand Corporation for development of outside opinions on its problems. Other services soon followed suit. Today there is a veritable industry surrounding Washington, DC, called "Beltway Bandits," which provides contractual services for the Department of Defense on some of its systems analysis problems.

8. Within the Department of Defense (DOD), the International Security Affairs agency was created in 1961. It has been regarded as a "Little State Department" within DOD. At the same time, within the Department of State, the Arms Control and Disarmament Agency and the Bureau of Politico-Military Affairs were created. Both seek to meld the military with the political in foreign policy.

9. *Report of the Commission on the Organization of the Government for the Conduct of Foreign Policy*, vol. 4, appendix K: *Adequacy of Current Organization: Defense and Arms Control*, by Robert D. Murphy, Chairman, is replete with case studies documenting the political pulling and hauling of the various "players" in the American weapons acquisition process.

10. If one defines cohesion as the ability of alliance partners to agree upon goals, strategy, and tactics, and to coordinate activities directed toward those ends, and efficacy as the ability of an alliance to achieve its goals, then the following analysts would link either new weapon technologies or technologically sophisticated hardware to NATO cohesion and efficacy: Thomas A. Callaghan, Jr., "A New North Atlantic Treaty of Technological Cooperation and Trade," in *NATO: The Next Thirty Years*, ed. Kenneth A. Meyers (Boulder, CO: Westview Press, 1980); Steven Canby, "The Alliance and Europe: Part IV, Military Doctrine and Technology," *Adelphi Papers*, No. 109 (London: International Institute for Strategic Studies, 1975); Waldo D. Freeman, *NATO Central Region Forward Defense: Correcting the Strategy/Force Mismatch* (Washington, DC: National Defense University Research Directorate, 1981); Lord Gladwyn, "The Defense of Western Europe," *Foreign Affairs* 51 (April 1973): 588; Kenneth Hunt, "Alternative Conventional Force Postures," in *NATO:The Next Thirty Years*, ed. Kenneth A. Meyers (Boulder, CO: Westview Press, 1980); Roger Morgan, "The Politics of European Defense Cooperation," in *Defense Politics in the Atlantic Alliance*, ed. Edwin H. Fedder (New York: Praeger Publishers, 1980); John H. Morse, "New Weapons Technologies: Implications for NATO," *Orbis* 19 (Summer 1975): 497; Robert Neild,

"European Self-Defense," *New York Times*, 17 February 1982, p. A-23; Johannes Steinhoff, "The Scope and Direction of New Weapons Technologies," in *New Conventional Weapons and East-West Security*, ed. Christoph Bertram (New York: Praeger Publishers, 1979).

11. See, for example, A. Rupert Hall and Norman Smith, eds., *History of Technology* (New York: Oxford University Press, 1961); Maurice Daumas, ed., *A History of Technology and Invention* (New York: Crown Publications, 1969); Elting E. Morison, *Men, Machines and Modern Times* (Cambridge: MIT Press, 1966).

12. Lynn Montross, *War Through the Ages*, 3rd ed. (New York: Harper and Row, 1960); P. E. Cleator, *Weapons of War* (New York: Thomas Y. Crowell Co., 1967); Theodore C. Mataxis and Seymour L. Goldberg, *Nuclear Tactics, Weapons and Firepower in the Pentomic Division, Battle Group and Company* (Harrisburg, PA: Military Service Publishing Co., 1958); I. B. Holley, Jr., *Ideas and Weapons* (New Haven: Yale University Press, 1953); George C. Reinhart and W. B. Kintner, *Atomic Weapons in Land Combat* (Harrisburg, PA: Military Service Publishing Co., 1954).

13. Cleator, *Weapons of War*; Walter Buehr, *Warrior's Weapons* (New York: Thomas Y. Crowell Co., 1963).

14. Holley, *Ideas and Weapons*.

15. There was a great deal of analysis of the effects of nuclear weapons on interstate relations in the late 1950s. These analyses will be discussed in greater detail in chapter 5.

16. Roger Facer, "The Alliance and Europe: Part IV, Weapons Procurement in Europe—Capabilities and Choices," *Adelphi Papers*, No. 108 (London: International Institute for Strategic Studies, 1975); D. C. R. Heyhoe, "The Alliance and Europe: Part IV, The European Programme Group," *Adelphi Papers*, No. 129 (London, International Institute for Strategic Studies, Winter 1976-1977); and Charles Wolf, Jr., and Derek Leebaert, "Trade Liberalization as a Path to Weapons Standardization in NATO," *International Security* 2 (Winter 1978): 136, are a few works on standardization of NATO hardware or "RSI" (Rationalization, Standardization, and Interoperability) as it has come to be known, in the period of the second case study.

17. Quincy Wright, *A Study of War*, 2nd ed. (Chicago: University of Chicago Press, 1965), pp. 313-14.

18. J. F. C. Fuller, *Armament and History* (New York: Charles Scribner's Sons, 1945), p. xiv.

19. Seyom Brown's *New Forces in World Politics* (Washington, DC: The Brookings Institution, 1974) is a succinct exposition of the dynamics of the international political system in the post–World War II era. Chapter 7 deals specifically with technology as a force for change in the world

order. Also, John Spanier, *Games Nations Play*, 3rd ed. (New York: Holt, Rinehart and Winston/Praeger, 1978), covers the changes resulting from technological forces.

20. Robert O. Keohane and Joseph S. Nye, *Power and Interdependence* (Boston: Little, Brown and Company, 1977), is perhaps the most widely read work on this subject.

21. See Joseph J. Kruzel, "The Preconditions and Consequences of Arms Control" (Ph.D. dissertation, Harvard University, 1974).

22. Many approaches to the study of the arms race phenomenon have been advanced. A comprehensive compilation of types of arms races, to include the action-reaction variety mentioned, appear in Colin S. Gray, "The Arms Race Phenomenon," *World Politics* 24 (October 1971): 39.

23. For a fuller treatment on the status of states belonging to NATO, see Edwin H. Fedder, *NATO: The Dynamics of Alliance in the Post-War World* (New York: Dodd, Mead and Company, 1973), chap. 4.

24. Alexander L. George and Richard Smoke, *Deterrence in American Foreign Policy: Theory and Practice* (New York: Columbia University Press, 1974), p. 95.

25. From n. 10, above, alliance cohesion was defined as the ability of alliance partners to agree upon goals, strategy, and tactics, and to coordinate activities directed toward those ends.

26. Appendix C of Ole R. Holsti, P. Terrence Hopmann, and John D. Sullivan, *Unity and Disintegration in International Alliances: Comparative Studies* (New York: John Wiley and Sons, 1973).

27. A note of caution about these propositions is in order. Some of the propositions were contradictory in nature, especially those dealing with the disintegration of alliances. This condition should not be viewed as a limitation of the method of research. Rather, it is more properly understood to be a result of the generally underdeveloped state of a comprehensive theory on alliances and the lack of systematic, comparable research in this area. Although not its primary concern, this work will address that condition.

28. An example of a proposition linking the status of the international political system to the cohesion of an alliance would be: "External danger causes allies to rally around alliance leaders." Arnold Wolfers, as cited in Holsti, Hopmann, and Sullivan, *Unity and Disintegration*, Appendix C.

29. An example of a proposition linking the attributes of alliance members to alliance performance would be: "Growing strength of minor alliance members may cause alliance dissension." Peter Calvocoressi, as cited in Holsti, Hopmann, and Sullivan, *Unity and Disintegration*, Appendix C.

2

Alliance Formation in the Postwar Era

The dawn of the aftermath of World War II was cold indeed. The war had produced a fundamental change in the structure and distribution of power in the international political system. Throughout Europe, economies and political systems once vibrant as the centers of world influence now lay debilitated by the war. The United States and the Soviet Union emerged from that conflict as the dominant states in what were to become their respective spheres of influence and as rivals in a contest to maintain those areas. Although wary partners during the war in a common effort to defeat Nazi Germany, the postwar era witnessed a hardening of the antagonisms between them. Opposing ideologies fostered incompatible, inimical belief systems; differing views of the future state system fostered suspicion and misperception of the other's foreign policy; and the bipolar distribution of power led each state to see the other as the principal threat to its security and to take steps which it saw as defensive but which were seen by the other as expansionistic and aggressive.[1] This conflict between the two rivals was particularly sharp in the vital European area.

AMERICAN INVOLVEMENT IN EUROPE

Europe's weakened status was a twofold problem for America. In its militarily and economically weak status, Western Europe was judged a liability for the United States. It was a resource prize which might sorely tempt a Soviet Union intent on rebuilding its own economic system and increasing the girth of its security belt. Yet it was an essential part of the security belt of the United States. America would have serious difficulty maintaining its security against the combined resources of Europe and Asia. To restore its vitality, then, and forestall any near-term Soviet aggressive intentions, Europe had to be revived economically and protected militarily. These twin concerns were clearly interrelated, since military security was essential to provide the climate of stability necessary for long-term economic investment and growth.

The initial economic response by the United States to Europe's problems was the grant of $400 million of economic aid and military supplies to the governments of Greece and Turkey in 1947. This program of assistance was broadened that summer to include aid for the majority of the nations of Europe through the Marshall Plan, the goal of which was the common economic recovery of Europe. Within three years of the plan's inception, Europe was exceeding its prewar production rate by 25 percent, inflation had been slowed, and the jobless rates were substantially reduced. The Marshall Plan was not without its economic benefits for America. It created an intense European demand for U.S.-produced goods, and, when combined with a system of fixed exchange rates pegged to the dollar price of gold, assured the United States the dominant position in the economic system of the West.

The efforts of the United States to establish firm economic foundations for Western stability must also be viewed against the backdrop of events which the West considered evidence of Soviet expansionistic tendencies. The danger engendered by the activities of the Soviet Union in supporting rebels in Greece, its pressures on Turkey and Iran, the Soviet-engineered coup in Czechoslovakia, and the Berlin blockade were clear enough signals to the West of hostile Soviet intentions. In an atmosphere of tension and insecurity produced by these events, there would be an obvious reluctance by the recipient governments of Marshall Plan aid to commit funds to long-term economic development. Too, in such an atmosphere the peoples of these states would be reluctant to make economic sacrifices or engage in investments, with economic stagnation and moribund growth the inevitable result. Military security, then, was a prerequisite for economic activity and development. Fearful of the new Soviet military moves for their own sake and cognizant of the need to provide a stable atmosphere conducive to economic growth, the states of Western Europe sought to promote their own security through mutual cooperation. Bilaterally at first, with the treaty of Dunkirk between England and France in 1947, and later on a more collective basis, the former wartime allies and foes sought to forge a military alliance to promote their national security.

Initially building upon their economic interactions, the nations of the Organization for European Economic Cooperation (OEEC) formed the military counterpart called the Brussels Pact.[2] Efforts by this group to attract American military support were successful, and in April 1949 Belgium, Canada, Denmark, France, Great Britain, Iceland, Italy, Luxemburg, Netherlands, Norway, Portugal, and the United States signed the NATO Treaty. The need for American participation in the alliance was clear. If the Soviets were to be deterred from attacking Western Europe, America's military and industrial capability had to be added to that of the members of the alliance. Without American military strength, NATO did not pose a credible war-fighting or deterrent capability.

THE CONTEXT FOR ALLIANCE FORMATION

The rationale of military security providing a fertile environment for economic development can be accurately identified as a motive for each state's membership in the alliance. However, this general consensus on the rationale for formation of NATO does not mean that all states conceived of their own particular requirements for national security in identical terms. Each state had its own perspectives on such matters. Those perspectives were largely a function of the individual state's political-military history, and political culture. These elements combined into what might be called a "strategic culture"—that is, the ideas, attitudes, expectations, and beliefs a state has about the military strategic goals it should pursue, the people and equipment (force structure) it should develop into forces, and the appropriate strategy required to manipulate that force structure to achieve those goals. As indicated, a state's "strategic culture" is particularistic in nature. Consequently, each state had its own peculiar motives for joining the alliance, its own intentions regarding the extent of its participation/contribution, and its own expectations about the purpose and operation of the alliance.

Strategic culture, in addition to providing the context for a state's military policies, is relatively slow to change. A state's attitudes and expectations can be affected by events, but such beliefs are deeply held, and as such, are not subject to change rapidly. In general, what is past is prologue; that which conditioned a state's actions previously is likely to be repeated in the future.

Let us turn to a brief discussion of the particular strategic perspectives of the major states of the alliance in order to understand better their orientation toward the alliance. Additionally, this discussion will provide a partial explanation of why states view differently the promise of new weapon technologies.[3]

American Strategic Culture

The American way of war reflected the peculiar American experience. Unlike most of the other NATO members, the United States had no war on its soil in any of its citizens' memories. It refrained from participation in the two World Wars for as long as possible, and when it finally became involved "over there," it was with grand goals: to "end all wars," and to "make the world safe for democracy." If America was to wage war, it was to be for clear-cut (and grand) objectives with a definite outcome (unconditional surrender) using all available resources, and would be accomplished quickly. When America waged war for poorly defined goals/objectives or with limited resources, as in Korea and later in Vietnam, popular disenchantment mounted.

Firepower was to be preferred over manpower; technology would substitute for the unpleasant part of wars, or perhaps preclude wars altogether. In part because of its fascination with technology and in part because of its global mission, the American defense establishment favored equipment that was designed to operate both in jungles and on tundras and, consequently, would too often do neither very well. Even during the limited wars in which it found itself, America's strategy generally reflected these concerns for equipment. In pursuit of Pancho Villa earlier in the century and subsequently in its war in Vietnam, Americans were never without supplies, ammunition, or fire support, making their efforts seem ponderous in comparison to a fleeting enemy.

Among its soldiers, ingenuity was prized. Commanders were expected to "be flexible," to "develop the situation," and to "use initiative." Although planning for war was to be detailed and thorough, its successful execution was largely the result of daring and drive on the part of the tactical commander. General George Patton's demonstration of the use of initiative and opportunism was (and remains) a favorite example in American military colleges for senior officers.

In sum, America preferred simple, quick, and definite solutions to its wars. Those solutions usually involved a preference for technology over manpower and favored a strategy of options that placed a premium on skillful blending of man and machine with decisive action to achieve a final outcome. Uncomfortable with uncertainty, Americans displayed a penchant for planning, yet would disregard the plan to seize the opportunity for "success."

British Strategic Culture

Britain had long been a European power, yet independent of the Continent. In the preceeding centuries, it had been British defense policy to maintain a military capability twice that of the most powerful Continental power, affording security from hostile alliances. If Britain did ally, such arrangements were entered into easily, and set aside just as easily by a "perfidious Albion." Relishing the independence afforded by its insular location, Britain was quite content to act as the external balancer to the Concert of Europe during the nineteenth century. As such, it was able to play a pivotal role in Continental politics without being a member of the Continent.

The British retrenchment in 1947 from the glory of the empire was painful. Nonetheless, substantial vestiges of that splendid past persisted. British appreciation for the deference paid to one of class was not easily lost—either domestically or internationally. Britain desired to retain that prestige, the distinction of the capacity to influence. If the circumstances/realities of the present age prevented it from being a dominant power, Britain would settle quite comfortably (for then) into the role of major power of the second order. Therefore, it embarked on a program of nuclear preparedness and the development of conventional forces. Those forces might not be as plentiful as those of a great power (the United States), but would be highly trained with first-rate equipment (although not as technologically sophisticated as that of a great power). Britain placed more reliance on the soldier than his equipment.

Among its soldiers, more stock was placed in making the best of a bad situation, of discipline and perseverance, of "toughing it out" than of abandoning a plan that was inadequate (the trench warfare of World War I, for example). Planning was to be conducted, but some things just could not be planned for, and must be "muddled through."

To recapitulate, British strategic culture called for a pivotal role for the British, even if that role was for a state not of the first rank. The British were reluctant to intertwine too closely their security with that of Europe's, and would prefer to retain a large measure of independence (or close association with the United States, perhaps to reap some of that prestige vicariously) if possible. Wartime strategies were to be developed and followed, although some things were better left unplanned. Forces might be small in number, but would be disciplined and confident, and be expected to "give a good account of themselves."

French Strategic Culture

Like Britain, French strategic policy underwent transformation after World War II, and contained some elements in common with British strategic policy. France, like Great Britain, had a glorious past as a great power and had a vision of greatness for itself in the future. Unlike Great Britain, this vision for the future placed France squarely in the pivotal position in Europe and, perhaps, the world.

Of Europe, France desired the role of arbitrator or dominant political authority in Europe.

French prominence required independence in defense policy and capability. That longing for military independence was fueled by France's humiliating defeat in World War II (and its subsequent experiences in Vietnam, Suez, and Algeria) and its perception of the Allies' slowness to liberate France. Such experiences caused France to view allies as unreliable, and enemies as implacable. For France the lesson was clear: it must have the independent ability to safeguard its interests.

Yet France could not, by itself, solve its security problems. Although France may have desired to be independent and to regain its past grandeur, its capabilities in the near term would not permit this. Its fear of the Soviet Union and a resurgent Germany were its two main preoccupations. If asked about its enemy, a French officer was likely to speak vaguely of "the enemy to the East," specifying neither Soviet nor German threat. In this century, French feelings toward the Germans have been clear. One may recall French Premier Georges Clemenceau's demands for the virtual dismantling of the German state after World War I, and French efforts at interweaving French and German heavy industry to preclude the capability of future German independence and to aid French economic development.

Like Britain, its pursuit of prominence would require France to seek security in an alliance. In the short term, this translated into action that secured French interests with minimal commitment. NATO was a suitable instrument for that policy. France saw its alliance role as thoughtful critic and cajoled others to follow its lead. In the long term, as circumstances permitted, France would disengage from NATO and seek the trappings of a great power— strategic nuclear weapons, tactical nuclear weapons, and conventional forces. It pursued these capabilities, but made no attempt to match the capabilities of the great powers, preferring instead to have a "proportionate capability" sufficient to dissuade an attack on French soil.

French plans and operations could be characterized by high sounding phrases of intent, but lackluster execution, especially against superior odds. The French psyche played a significant role in the French military. When the battle went well, French zeal was abundant. Once reversed, however, regaining that zeal proved difficult, with attendant consequences in the near term.

To review, French strategic culture called for France to play the pivotal leadership role in Europe. The temporary relapse of French capability, as occurred because of World Wars I and II, could be compensated for by alliance politics until France was prepared to assume its rightful role. Accomplishing this mission of leadership "from the Atlantic to the Urals" would require France to be capable of independent action, with appropriate forces and strategy. When capable militarily and psychologically of fulfilling that role, France would lead by example and cajole others into following.

German Strategic Culture

The common thread which flowed through German policy, especially defense policy, was the notion of restraint. Due mainly to the events of World War II, Germany found itself (and endeavors to keep itself) in a state of balance between opposing forces. The forces were both international and domestic in origin and were political, military, and economic in nature. Internationally, Germany was incapable of defending itself against the twice-invaded Soviets and relied upon the American strategic guarantee. Additionally, an independent Germany with military capability outside the structures of the NATO alliance, or a Germany providing a significantly lower proportionate contribution of troops and other resources to the alliance was unacceptable to most NATO members.

The amount of German participation in the alliance had domestic constraints. German leadership was overly concerned with domestic order and hence reluctant to pursue expensive or controversial military policies. Higher defense costs would provoke inflation and eat into social welfare programs; controversial programs would invite social unrest—all of which invoked unpleasant memories of Germany unrestrained. Germany's punishment for its World War II actions would be to shoulder much of the resource burden of the alliance in order to threaten the Soviets, yet not the Belgians.

The German military was well known for its meticulous planning, and deservedly so. Ingenuity and hard work remained the hallmarks of German military operations. Thorough training and preparation were routine. Planned operations were limited in geographic scope; no plans were made for sweeping, offensive operations (as were favored in World Wars I and II). Instead, a tight defense of the homeland was favored.

Because of its geographic location, Germany did not desire a strategy which envisioned a long conflict. Such a war promised to devastate the German countryside or to trade that countryside for the time required for the alliance to commit more forces to stem the battle. Therefore, Germany's preference was for deterrence of war by threatening the attacker with maximum punishment. If war did come, it was to be violent and ended as rapidly as possible. Given the international and domestic restrictions on the development of its forces, Germany had little choice but to opt for security within the context of NATO, and for a strategy that placed a premium on maintaining the territorial integrity of Germany itself.

With such diversity in the various beliefs and expectations about alliance functioning by the major members, one might well expect long-term diversity in the judgments of all the members regarding their alliance orientation and their commitment to it. Indeed, such has been the case, as will be identified throughout these case studies.

THE STRENGTHENING OF THE ALLIANCE

By the end of the 1940s, the relations between the U.S. and the U.S.S.R. could accurately be described as a "Cold War," yet NATO had not blossomed into the full-fledged military instrument it was to become. Initially, the alliance was a traditional one—it had no military leaders, it controlled no military forces, it had no military strategy, and it had no logistical or administrative base.[4] Troops in Germany as a part of occupation duty by the British, French, and Americans, were scattered about in small groups and were mostly untrained young men who had no battle experience. The fledgling alliance had but one-tenth the number of operational airfields needed to support those troops. The supply lines from the United States ran not across France from the protected English

Channel, but close to and parallel to the expected front lines—south from Bremerhaven and Hamburg.

The alliance, then, was not on an operational footing. It was only a written agreement to consult and react in the event of hostilities.[5] Additionally, it was thought that the small amount of conventional forces then in existence belonging to the member nations and the Strategic Air Command (SAC) of the United States with its nuclear capability would be sufficient to deter Soviet aggression in Europe. In the unlikely event deterrence failed, NATO's military strategy (such as it was), was to avoid the cycle of destruction, occupation, and liberation. Conventional forces, supplied in the main by the European members of the alliance, were to hold the invading Communist forces at bay while the strategic bombing forces of SAC would blunt the Soviet attack and reduce the urban-industrial complex of the Soviet homeland to rubble.[6]

While underdeveloped and certainly not on an operational footing, NATO was America's means for the defense of Europe. That its strategy was suspect at best was not troubling to the Truman administration, since the atomic weapons in America's arsenal were judged sufficient to deter the Soviet Union. But subsequent events were to shake that confidence.

The unexpectedly rapid Soviet progress in the development of an atomic bomb, the "loss" of China to the Communists in 1949, and, soon after, the North Korean attack to the south caused concern among administration officials that "monolithic communism" was on the march and would not be deterred solely by America's atomic capability. A "means" must be constructed to meet the challenge of containment. The rationale for that "means" was provided by the American National Security Council in the summer of 1950. Called NSC-68, this report was a comprehensive statement of national interests, threats to those interests, and feasible responses. Communicated throughout the bureaucracy, NSC-68 was to sound the war tocsin; it was a call to military preparedness. It summarized the Western vulnerabilities, advocated quick responses to all instances of Communist attempts to make gains, and called for the strengthening of America's military alliances.

Europe's response to the events described above was an attempt to invigorate NATO and transform it into an operational peacetime military command. The overall Allied military commander in World War II, General Dwight D. Eisenhower, was appointed Supreme Allied Commander in Europe and head of the military formations of the alliance. Command structures were established and a forward defense strategy was inaugurated. As the "police action" in Korea wore on, concern mounted that the military actions there were a feint and that the real thrust by the Communists would be in Europe. Consequently, as a result of American urging, members of the alliance agreed in Lisbon in 1952 to increase their total of conventional forces able to deploy in thirty days from sixteen divisions to an astonishing ninety-six divisions.[7] The strategy for their employment was to be that of "tripwire"— that is, a device to assure an American response to Soviet aggression. The divisions were to hold the advancing Soviet forces at the Elbe River (the forward defense concept called the "shield"), while the nuclear "sword" of the American SAC laid waste to the Russian homeland.

It was at this juncture that the North Atlantic Alliance took on a life of its own. The alliance had been transformed from a written commitment by the signatories to cooperate in time of war into an operational military command with a concept for operation, the (promised) resources to carry out those operations, and, most importantly, the direction to conduct operational planning and training during peacetime. It was this novel aspect of regularized, integrated, military operations during peacetime that made these plans for the NATO alliance unique. Unlike past alliances which were formed as a response to war or functional only during wartime, the NATO alliance in time of peace was to prepare for war. Such broad planning goals were, however, difficult to meet in reality.

MATCHING MEANS WITH ENDS— THE "NEW LOOK"

Europe of the 1950s was still a war-weary Europe. Although the Marshall Plan had been of great assistance in reviving the economies of Europe, the process was not at all complete. The European states of the alliance were heavily engaged in the process of economic recovery and were still politically weak. As such, within a year it became clear they could not achieve the lofty military goals of the Lisbon Conference. For the European nations, it was the age-old question of guns or butter. Resources committed to production and purchase of weapons could not be used to increase a state's standard of living. In most states, the priority of production went to the "butter."

The United States also faced fundamental policy choices in 1953. The Korean War had been expensive and the policy of containment inherent in the NSC-68 document did not adequately address the problem of matching "means" with "ends."[8] Under that policy, all threats to America were of equal importance and to be met with appropriate forces. Hence, force requirements skyrocketed. Psychologically, the war had not had a wholly satisfactory outcome for the United States, which left a distaste in America's mouth for "limited wars."[9] For America, the notion of fighting with only a portion of its resources committed to the war in an effort to achieve something less than "total victory" was new and seemingly foolish. Americans yearned for a dynamic strategy that took full advantage of the technological superiority of American's weaponry—but which would do so at a reduced cost. Burdened by the financial costs of two wars in twelve years, the new Republican administration sought ways to ease military spending, yet provide military security for America and its allies in a dynamic fashion. Immediately upon assuming office in 1953, it conducted a review of America's defense strategy, which resulted in the promulgation of a series of new policies. The "New Look," as these policies were known, sought to address specifically the issues raised above.

AMERICAN DEFENSE STRATEGY AND NATO

The "New Look" was a comprehensive dramatic turnabout from Truman's policies. Deterrence by threat of massive unlimited punishment was to replace Truman's containment of aggression by war fighting. The initiative for executing this strategy would now rest with the United States, rather than with Truman's response-oriented strategy. Lastly, this policy was to be cheaper than

Truman's. These three factors were woven together into what was a conscious attempt to match ends, means, and domestic political realities in the development of policy.

The military strategy of the "New Look" came to be known as Massive Retaliation and embodied these three factors of deterrence, initiative, and economy.[10] Explicitly, the potential aggressor was forewarned that he might suffer retaliation by American nuclear weapons as a consequence of his aggression. Fearing such consequences, the aggressor was to be deterred. The initiative for this strategy was to reside with the United States, since it controlled the employment of the weapons and it could thereby select the means and places of its response to the aggression. Rather than allow the opponent to select the battlefield and the weapons, the United States would no longer be bound by such restrictions. "Limited wars" would be limited only because the United States chose to keep them so. Henceforth, the options of escalation were the province of the United States. Economy of resources was a direct by-product of the above two factors.

By relying on the means of mass destruction to deter aggression, large, costly troop deployments to counter the enemy no longer were required.[11] The Air Force, with its planes and bombs, was less costly than an Army and was to be the major means of deterrence. Additionally, redeployments of Army forces, especially those in the peripheral areas such as Asia, could be made to the United States to form the basis of a strategic reserve. This reserve could be transported to potential trouble spots, as required. The continental basing of troops would save money and, by being centrally located in the United States, the selection of "places of our choosing" could more easily be made. Deployment to either Asia or Europe would be equally rapid. As a consequence of this new policy, the American military planned for fewer troops and more aircraft in developing its forces. It could do so, since it had received assurances that tactical and strategic nuclear weapons would be readily available if required in combat. America's allies, both in Europe and in Asia, were asked to provide the bulk of local conventional ground capabilities, which would be backed by local U.S. military assistance. These allies were also to provide the bases for use by SAC aircraft as staging areas until intercontinental-range delivery systems became available.

President Eisenhower did not desire to maintain large numbers of conventional forces abroad for the purpose of fighting a large-scale conventional war in Europe or Asia, yet he doubted that the United States could rely on its allies to contribute substantial levels of conventional forces to meet the Lisbon force goals. The economic problems of America were not unique; Europe suffered from the same inability to match means with ends. If the United States could use technology at the strategic level, perhaps the same principles were applicable at the tactical level.

Just as technology was the catalyst for the Industrial Revolution, which replaced men with machines, technology would replace men in the NATO alliance with firepower. Nuclear weapons, which had been successful in causing Japan to capitulate in World War II at a projected saving of over one million Allied soldiers' lives, would again substitute for soldiers. Because of advances in physics and nuclear engineering, by 1953 it was possible to produce nuclear weapons with small yields which would permit their use on the tactical battlefield. These tactical nuclear weapons, then, were to be the solution to the problems of the member nations of the alliance. By substituting firepower for manpower the alliance could develop the requisite amount of military capability, but at a fraction of the financial cost. These weapons were to have political power also. Within the administration, the power of tactical nuclear weapons as a diplomatic tool had been shown. Eisenhower, upon assuming the U.S. presidency during the stalemated portion of the Korean War, "passed the word" that the United States was prepared to employ tactical nuclear weapons in Korea in order to break the stalemated talks.[12] Since the North Koreans/Red Chinese hurriedly came to terms, to many Americans especially, the coercive power of nuclear weapons had been proved. Thus, to compensate for anticipated cuts in U.S. conventional force strength, the Eisenhower administration's basic defense policy from the outset called for reliance on tactical nuclear weapons as well as strategic nuclear forces. Selective retaliation by localized nuclear forces was to supplement the massive retaliation by the strategic forces. Nuclear weapons of both the strategic and tactical category were thus basic to the concepts of the "New Look." This concept for the employment of nuclear weapons brought a public reaction that was both rapid and vocal. The reasons for the concern will become more apparent after a brief description of the nature of tactical nuclear weapons.

NOTES

1. The evolution of the Cold War era is taken from John Lewis Gaddis, *The United States and the Origins of the Cold War, 1941-1947* (New York: Columbia University Press, 1972), pp. 353-61; John W. Spanier, *American Foreign Policy Since World War II*, 9th ed. (New York: Holt, Rinehart and Winston, 1983), pp. 15-23 and 37-38; Charles W. Kegley, Jr., and Eugene R. Wittkopf, *American Foreign Policy: Pattern and Process* (New York: St. Martin's Press, 1982), pp. 50-56; Joan Edelman Spero, *The Politics of International Economic Relations* (New York: St. Martin's Press, 1977), pp. 31-35; U.S. Department of State, American Foreign Policy 1950-1955, *Basic Documents*, Pub.: 6446 (1957), p. 829; and Alan K. Henrikson, "The Creation of the North Atlantic Alliance," *Naval War College Review* 32 (May/June 1980): 14-16.

2. Treaty efforts by Europe and the United States are from Spanier, *American Foreign Policy Since World War II*, pp. 38-39.

3. Three points concerning the discussions of strategic culture must be made at the outset. First, these discussions are only of the major states of Central Europe. Discussions of the smaller, less powerful states of the alliance have been omitted because their policies are largely bound up in the policies pursued by their more powerful neighbors. Second, because a state's strategic culture is not subject to change rapidly, I have been content to cite some examples of the strategic culture that occurred subsequent to the formation of NATO. While chronologically inconsistent, the substance of the argument is, I believe, unaffected. Lastly, it is recognized that West Germany did not become a member of NATO in 1949. However, German participation in NATO was soon thereafter a topic for discussion, and Germany was admitted to membership in 1955. The discussion of German strategic culture is included out of historical context primarily for stylistic reasons.

4. This section on the invigoration of the NATO alliance is taken from Roger Hilsman, "On NATO Strategy," in *Alliance Policy in the Cold War*, ed. Arnold Wolfers (Baltimore: Johns Hopkins University Press, 1959), p. 146; Spanier, *American Foreign Policy Since World War II*, p. 39; Henrikson, "The Creation of the North Atlantic Alliance," pp. 29-31; and Huntington, *The Common Defense* (New York: Columbia University Press, 1961), pp. 312-24.

5. In the United States, there was great reluctance to commit large numbers of American troops to the defense of Europe even with the NATO agreement. Within the U.S. Senate, Senator Arthur S. Vandenberg led a group which was extremely reluctant to allow American involvement in Europe's affairs. See Henrikson, "The Creation of the North Atlantic Alliance," p. 22.

6. John Lewis Gaddis, *Strategies of Containment* (New York: Oxford University Press, 1982), chaps. 5 and 6: Henrikson, "The Creation of the North Atlantic Alliance," pp. 26-28; and Hilsman, "On NATO Strategy," pp. 147-48.

7. Hilsman, "On NATO Strategy," p. 150.

8. Gaddis, *Strategies*, chap. 4; and Huntington, *The Common Defense*, p. 164.

9. Spanier, *American Foreign Policy Since World War II*, p. 169.

10. Information on the policy of Massive Retaliation is from Huntington, *The Common Defense*, pp. 64-68; Glenn H. Snyder, "The 'New Look' of 1953," in *Strategy, Politics and Defense Budgets*, ed. Warner R. Schilling, Paul Y. Hammond, and Glenn H. Snyder, (New York: Columbia University Press, 1962); and Gaddis, *Strategies*, chap. 6. The policy of Massive Retaliation will be discussed in greater detail in subsequent chapters.

11. The military capabilities acquired by the United States and the strategy for their employment during the Eisenhower years reflected the guidance contained in NSC-68/2. See Seyom Brown, *The Faces of Power: Constancy and Change in U.S. Foreign Policy from Truman to Johnson* (New York: Columbia University Press, 1968), pp. 72-73; Gaddis, *Strategies*, chap. 6; and Jerome H. Kahn, *Security in the Nuclear Age* (Washington, DC: The Brookings Institution, 1975), chap. 1.

12. Dwight D. Eisenhower, *The White House Years*, vol. I: *Mandate for Change* (New York: Doubleday, 1963), pp. 178-81.

3

Tactical Nuclear Weapons

The NATO alliance had been formed by the states of Western Europe out of a concern for Soviet aggressive intentions. The United States was initially a reluctant partner in this group, but as events in Korea unfolded and as the Soviet Union joined the United States as a nuclear power, America's political commitment to the alliance grew. Matching the means with that commitment proved difficult for all alliance members, however. The efforts involved with rebuilding the states' political and economic structures left little money for military forces. Lofty, perhaps unrealistic, force structure goals went unmet as the alliance members sought to regain their budgetary and monetary health.

In an attempt to alleviate the deficiency in military capabilities, in 1953 the United States offered the use of a new weapons technology. Small yield and short-range tactical nuclear weapons were hailed as a means of providing firepower with less manpower. The nuclear genie, as it had solved Allies' needs in World War II, could rescue them again. Now packaged in a tactical bottle, it was believed that this atomic wonder could provide the needed "beef up to NATO's punch," but at much less cost than conventional forces.[1] The awesome military effectiveness of nuclear weapons had been demonstrated in World War II, but the specific characteristics of these weapons and their military and political implications were largely unknown or not fully understood. It would be useful, then, to review the cost, availability, and proposed strategy for use of this new technology in an effort to assess its full impact on NATO.

THE TACTICAL NUCLEAR WEAPON PRICE TAG

Human military forces are expensive to field. They must be selected, inducted, trained, fed, equipped, and paid on a recurring basis. After their service, they must be pensioned off. Mechanical forces, however, are different. Once research, development, and procurement costs are paid, the costs of operating these devices are normally decidedly lower than those for human resources. Tactical nuclear weapons are no exception.

Although the actual cost of a tactical nuclear bomb remains classified as a military secret, a rough estimate would be $1 million each. Although this is certainly not inexpensive, it is clearly cheaper than the monetary and social costs of fielding one armored division (approximately fifteen thousand soldiers) for a year.[2] Additionally, since a nuclear weapon is not consumed during its existence, there is no recurring replacement cost as there is for a body of troops. Granted, tactical nuclear weapons must be maintained, secured, and periodically updated, but this cost is still far below that for conventional forces. Too, the social costs for nuclear weapons are not nearly as expensive as those associated with a conscript force. Also, manpower not utilized by the armed forces is available as labor in the economic sector. Therefore, for budgetary and social reasons, member states of NATO were attracted to the idea of the substitution of firepower via tactical nuclear weapons for the manpower of conventional forces. But this end-item cost is somewhat deceptive. The highest cost of the development of nuclear weapons is in their research and development, when the tremendous expense of construction of facilities, start-up costs, working models, design costs, and trial and error experimentation is incurred.[3]

The United States previously had absorbed much of these costs during its effort to develop strategic nuclear weapons in World War II. The carry-over of the technology developed for strategic nuclear weapons aided the development of tactical nuclear weapons. For another country to attempt the development of tactical nuclear weapons without American technological assistance, the costs would have been much greater. Additionally, the number of technically capable personnel available worldwide to work on the project was severely limited, as was the availability of uranium, the fissionable material of the bomb.[4] These drawbacks virtually precluded other alliance members from attempting to produce tactical nuclear weapons without the assistance of the United States. Since the diversion of resources from the non-military sector of the economy for the fielding of additional forces was proving to be politically impossible, it was hardly likely that the needed massive resources would be diverted for use in the development of nuclear weapons. Additionally, members reasoned that since the United States possessed the capability to deter the Soviets, why should they need to duplicate that capability? For the reasons of high initial cost, scarce technology and resources (both human and material), and their seemingly senseless duplication of deterrent effort, other member nations of NATO did not pursue this new technology for themselves.

THE AVAILABILITY OF TACTICAL NUCLEAR WEAPONS

That its allies did not attempt to pursue the development of nuclear weapons technology was certainly consistent with U.S. aims. The United States had no desire to share (and by law could not share) its atomic monopoly with other nations. The exception was Great Britain, with which the United States had a "special relationship" by virtue of its World War II cooperation on the Manhattan Project. Immediately after World War II, the United States had taken steps ostensibly to further arms control, but in reality to consolidate its position as the sole possessor of the nuclear capability. The Baruch plan, proposed by the United States in 1946, sought to freeze existing development of nuclear technology under the control of an international authority. American bomb production, however, was not to be limited during the four or five years it would take to constitute this international authority.[5]

Once operational, this authority would call for the dismantling of bombs and the factories used in their production. Research for the peaceful application of the uses of nuclear energy would be carried out under the auspices of this international authority. Violators of the plan's ban on manufacturing nuclear weapons were to be subject to sanctions applied independently of any United Nations veto. The Soviet Union, as a "have not" nation, rejected this plan for two reasons. It denied the Soviets the possibility to develop strategic nuclear weapons as the United States possessed, and it required on-site inspections to which the Soviets had always objected. With the rejection of the Baruch plan, the United States made no further offers of disarmament.

Domestically, the United States had taken steps to limit the dissemination of information pertaining to the development and production of nuclear weapons. The Atomic Energy Act of 1946 specifically prohibited any kind of international cooperation and forbade the dissemination of any data "concerning the manufacture, utilization of atomic weapons, the production of fissionable material, or the use of fissionable materials in the production" under punishment of death.[6]

In summary, this new technology was expensive, difficult to develop, and America had no intention of sharing its control with its allies. Nuclear weapons remained the exclusive province of the United States. Possession of this military technology placed a great burden upon the United States for its prudent use, but it also provided the United States with a trump card in the organization and operation of the alliance.

TACTICAL NUCLEAR WEAPONS AND NATO STRATEGY

As indicated in the previous chapter, the 1952 Lisbon call to infuse NATO with conventional divisions for defense of the old Western front soon proved to be an insurmountable task. Neither the economies nor the political systems of any of the states of the alliance could support such an endeavor. Besides, the prospect of more efficient tactical nuclear weapons and America's pledge of its strategic bombers made the task seem less immediate. This was due partly to the manner in which America's strategic doctrine—Massive Retaliation—was announced and the controversy which immediately surrounded it. In revealing the new policy in January 1954, the American secretary of state, John Foster Dulles, seemed to indicate that the capacity to retaliate massively was to be the primary means for defense of all areas, not mainly Europe.[7] Nor did the secretary adequately address the need for local forces, even in Europe, to combat aggression in its early stages. Therefore, it seemed that all instances of aggression were either to be permitted by the United States or turned into a general nuclear war. It was denied that this was the intent of the "New Look" or of Massive Retaliation, but it certainly was implied in the policy decisions and actions of the United States.[8]

In accordance with the dictates of "economy" and "initiative," any conflicts larger than "brush fires" or border incidents were to be considered nuclear for military planning purposes. If limitations were to be observed, they would be a function of the size or yield of the nuclear weapons. By employing nuclear weapons, the number of American troops needed to fight wars could similarly be kept limited. Consequently, budget requests prepared at this time reflected decreases in American manpower, especially in the Army.

The controversy over this new policy was almost immediate. Within the United States it concentrated mainly on the perception that all instances of aggression were to be deterred by the threat of massive nuclear strikes against the enemy. This was attacked on two counts. First, such a threat in all but the most serious of circumstances was believed not credible. The prospect of the use of American nuclear weapons had not deterred the North Koreans in 1950, nor would it do so except in the case of a most serious threat in Europe. Second, if deterrence failed, was the United States prepared to risk escalation to general nuclear war on behalf of anything less than war in Europe?

For Europe, confusion was immediately apparent. What was "new" about the "New Look," unless it was the matter of choice inherent in the phrase "time and place of our choosing"? The linkage of SAC to war in Europe had always been agreed upon. Now the element of choice was raised. When coupled with the notion of a redeployment of ground forces to America as part of a strategic reserve and the already announced reductions in overall American Army strength, the concerns of Europe were present, but muted. Although the United States repeatedly pledged its strategic support for Europe, the seeds of doubt had been planted. Even so, the arrival of tactical nuclear weapons in Europe in 1954 and the continued pledges of the United States to provide its strategic sword gave Europe the rationale it needed to reduce its conventional forces in expectation of a very brief fight before the arrival of SAC.

These reductions and the anticipated further decrease in manpower requirements allowed by the infusion of tactical nuclear weapons made it increasingly necessary to revise the military strategy of NATO.[9] NATO military commanders feared that any governmental permission to employ nuclear weapons might be received too late to be of any benefit. They became apprehensive that war in Europe would therefore find them with neither the troops nor the nuclear weapons as a substitute. Not wishing to be faced with those unfortunate choices, senior NATO military officials began to agitate publicly for a revision to the military strategy of NATO. If tactical nuclear weapons were now part of the alliance, then a military strategy governing their employment was also required. Accordingly, in December 1954, in anticipation of further reductions to the number of forces then under the control of NATO, the governing North Atlantic Council gave permission to the military to revise its strategy and base its planning on the use of tactical nuclear weapons.[10] The results of those changes to the military strategy will be examined later.

In order to understand why tactical nuclear weapons were later to cause divisions within NATO, it is necessary to review something of the nature of nuclear weapons. As a new technology, they were fundamentally different from the existing body of weapons. The nature of those differences and their practical effects require examination.

THE NATURE OF TACTICAL NUCLEAR WEAPONS

Thus far, the discussion of tactical nuclear weapons and NATO has focused on the imprecise term of "firepower." Concentration on "firepower" neglects some of the more critical aspects of nuclear weapons. Let us turn to a closer examination of the physical and, more importantly, politically significant implications of this new technology. This examination obviously must be cursory and somewhat untechnical; it assumes the reader is familiar with the general physical effects of nuclear explosions. However, such an examination is central to the development of this case study. By understanding some of the novel characteristics of nuclear explosions, a clearer appreciation for their political ramifications may be gained. It was precisely these political ramifications which were to bedevil the alliance. The implications of this new weapon technology will be divided into three categories: force structuring (the manning and equipping of units), collateral damage by blast and radiation, and political signaling (the conveyance of political intentions by political or non-political events).

The great increase in firepower provided by nuclear weapons over that of conventional explosives led some analysts in the early 1950s to foresee a decreased logistics support requirement.[11] Tanks, artillery, and the people to operate and maintain those expensive pieces of equipment would be needed in far fewer numbers because the equivalent amount of firepower could be provided by a few tactical nuclear weapons. The reduction in manpower (with all its associated costs of pay, pensions, training, feeding, housing, and social deprivation) and the attendant life-cycle costs of initial purchase, spare parts, and maintenance facilities promised by tactical nuclear weapons was very attractive to alliance members, especially during a period when domestic economic concerns were increasingly effective claimants on national budgets.

But the increase in firepower was not to be "cost free." Because of their tremendous power, nuclear explosions can cause extensive damage. Even though considered "small" in comparison to the yields employed in strategic weapons, tactical nuclear weapons with the equivalent of ten thousand tons of TNT could still produce extensive damage, especially if employed in built-up areas. Therefore, what was classed as "tactical" or "small" in one sense might appear to be "strategic" when viewed in terms of the destruction caused. Within the alliance, what seemed to Americans to be tactical (read "small yield," "selective employment") use of a nuclear weapon, would be an awesomely destructive strategic weapon to a German or a Belgian if it were employed there. Clearly one might well be reluctant to employ "only" tactical nuclear weapons if it meant the destruction of one's society. Although labeled a tactical nuclear weapon, depending upon one's proximity to the blast, the weapon's designation might well be meaningless amid the rubble.

Another aspect of collateral damage was the radiation caused by a nuclear explosion. Militarily, it might be desirable to contaminate an area with radiation in order to deny it to enemy use. In so doing, however, one would also deny it to friendly use. The duration of the period of denial could vary from a few hours to many hundreds of years, depending upon the nature of the explosion. Since the actual employment of nuclear weapons is not at all a precise science, the period of contamination for an area cannot be calculated with any certainty. Clearly, when used within one's territorial boundaries, contamination takes on heightened importance. Another more far-reaching problem associated with nuclear weapon radiation is fallout. The debris picked up by the fireball of a nuclear explosion will be contaminated by the radioactive particles of the weapon's fissionable material and will be transported via the prevailing winds a distance from the explosion site. Hence, non-combatants or even non-belligerents might receive potentially lethal doses of radioactivity for a period (perhaps years) after the explosion. The effects of the war would thus be widened, causing greater political complications.

The apparent lack of distinction between tactical and strategic employment of nuclear weapons was to provoke other problems as well. As a means of signaling observance of political restraints, nuclear weapons had distinct shortcomings. The yield of a nuclear weapon is dependent upon a number of factors, but to some degree can be fixed at almost any amount. There exists, however, a certain variance in the intended and actual yield of the explosion. Also, the exact size of the yield of a nuclear explosion is difficult to determine from visual observation. Although the diameter of the fireball does vary with the yield of the explosion, such a relationship is quite inexact and is not a reliable guide to determine yield size. Since it is quite difficult to determine the yield of an explosion, using yield size as a demonstration of adherence to political limitations during wartime is not possible. For example, it may not be possible to demonstrate restraint or keep a conflict "limited" by using only ten kiloton weapons or less.[12] The communication of adherence to that limitation to the enemy is not possible when attempting to use the observed size of the blast as the medium. Some other method must be employed.

The bright light and radiation emission of a nuclear blast are two other characteristics which are related to the problem of demonstrating restraint. Because of these two distinctive "signature effects," the detonation of a nuclear weapon is unmistakable and cannot be confused with that of a conventional explosion. Thus the symbolic value of the initial employment of nuclear weapons is clear—the user has escalated the conflict. However, because of the continuous variability in yield and the inability of an observer to determine accurately the size of the yield, the most distinct symbolic value of tactical nuclear weapons seemed to be in their non-use. Once used, nuclear weapons themselves possessed no further unique, mutually observable boundary in their employment.[13] The twin characteristics of continuous yield variability and the distinctive signature effect of a nuclear weapon were to cause great debate within the alliance as it wrestled with the problems of employing nuclear weapons as policy instruments of influence—that is, for their political effect. The purpose of the threat or use of military force is to achieve one's political goals. If the intended effect of a particular policy instrument (such as tactical nuclear weapons) is likely to be misunderstood, then at the very least, the terms and conditions of its employment will be debatable. And so it was in NATO, as we shall see.

In summary, tactical nuclear weapons heralded mixed effects for the NATO alliance. Their great firepower was thought to be the means whereby standing military establishments and, hence, economic costs could be reduced. This same power, however, would produce devastating damage at the area of employment. Since yield sizes could be varied along a continuum with no convenient, readily identifiable boundaries, the political use of tactical nuclear weapons as instruments of communication and influence was difficult. The most effective mode of employment seemed to some to be non-employment.

But both sides of the tactical nuclear coin were not as clear as they appear to be now. Hindsight has provided a better vantage point than was available in the mid 1950s, when the utility of tactical nuclear weapons for NATO was being discussed.[14] The tendency to overemphasize the military utility of tactical nuclear weapons as a means to reduce military spending, and the lack of debate about the political implications of tactical nuclear weapons for NATO prior to their introduction, were to cause the actual effect of that new technology to be quite different than was expected. The nature of the debate about tactical nuclear weapons within NATO, their relation to the environment of NATO, and an overall assessment of the actual effect of tactical nuclear weapons on NATO remain to be discussed.

NOTES

1. Phraseology commonly used by the U.S. Department of Defense at that time.

2. It is estimated that the equipment and supplies needed to outfit the four U.S. divisions requested at the Lisbon Conference would have cost $40-50 billion, even then. This figure does not include pay, housing, and rations for the forces. Nor is there any acceptable way to measure the costs of individual deprivations caused by the involuntary drafting of citizens. See Alain C. Enthoven and K. Wayne Smith, *How Much Is Enough?* (New York: Harper and Row, 1971; Harper Colophon, 1972), pp. 119-20. Compare this figure with the entire United States Department of Defense Budget of FY1950 of $13 billion. Source: The Budget of the United States Government for the Fiscal Year Ending 30 June 1955, p. M37, as quoted in Samuel P. Huntington, *The Common Defense* (New York: Columbia University Press, 1961), p. 209.

3. For a good appreciation of the scope and scale of the American effort to produce nuclear weapons during and after World War II, see Corbin Allardice and Edward R. Trapnell, *The Atomic Energy Commission* (New York: Praeger Publishers, 1974), chaps. 1-2.

4. See Warner R. Schilling, "The H-Bomb Decision: How to Decide Without Actually Choosing," *Political Science Quarterly* 76 (March 1961):24, for a discussion on the opportunity costs of diverting plutonium from production of atomic (fission) devices to fusion devices. The article describes the limited availability of personnel and of fissionable material in the early stages of their production of America's nuclear arsenal.

5. Information on the Baruch plan is taken from George H. Quester, *Nuclear Diplomacy* (New York: The Dunellen Publishing Co., Inc., 1970), pp. 18-21.

6. Section 10(b) (1) of the Atomic Energy Act of 1946, as quoted in Allardice and Trapnell, *Commission*, p. 32.

7. Much discussion developed within the U.S. government as to the roles of the three major services in supporting Massive Retaliation. This discussion provides insight into the specifics of how the administration (at least initially) conceptualized the nature of deterrence. Glenn Snyder reports that in the draft of the policy paper on the "New Look" the president desired the Air Force to be considered "*the* deterrent means." The Army, Navy, and defense secretary felt the paper should characterize the Air Force as "*a major* deterrent means." The president compromised to permit the use of the phrase "*the major* deterrent means." This was not a small semantic change; it reflected a vast gulf between the president and portions of his military staff in the concept of deterrence and foreshadowed the weaknesses of the new policy as it was to emerge. See Glenn H. Snyder, "The 'New Look' of 1953," in *Strategy, Politics and Defense Budgets*, ed. Warner R. Schilling, Paul Y. Hammond, and Glenn H. Snyder (New York: Columbia University Press, 1962), p. 437.

8. One policy decision taken early in the Eisenhower administration which was to fuel doubts about the viability of ground combat forces in the "New Look" was the reduction of the Army's budget by $4.1 billion in total Defense-wide cut of $4.8 billion. This represented a reduction in the Defense budget of 10 percent and nearly a 20 percent reduction of the Army's budget. Army personnel strength was reduced by 33 percent from December 1953 to June 1955. Such cuts were not universally endorsed by the Department of Defense. As indicated in the previous note, disagreement existed within the administration as to the proper means for effecting deterrent policy. The secretary of state and the president believed that the threat of the use of strategic nuclear weapons would suffice in all circumstances, except in the most minor cases of aggression. The Army (and its chief of staff, General Ridgeway, in particular) and the Navy felt that other, less massive applications of force would be required in order actually to consummate the threat. Both sides were, at least in the initial phases of the development of Massive Retaliation, concentrating on the "means" aspects of deterrence. It was on this point of credibility that Massive Retaliation as a deterrent to all levels of conflict was most vulnerable. For a good discussion of the "New Look" and the American attempt to match ends with means, see John Lewis Gaddis, *Strategies of Containment* (New York: Oxford University Press, 1982), chaps. 5 and 6. Data listed above on budgets and personnel are from chap. 6.

9. Roger Hilsman, "On NATO Strategy," in *Alliance Policy in the Cold War*, ed. Arnold Wolfers (Baltimore: Johns Hopkins University Press, 1959), p. 151.

10. The text of the communique issued by the Council may be found in *Department of State Bulletin*, 3 January 1955, p. 10.

11. The prediction of reduced logistical requirements brought about by substituting nuclear weapons for men and material was behind the Eisenhower administration's acceptance of the "New Look" reliance on nuclear weapons in the early 1950s. Huntington, *The Common Defense*, (New York: Columbia University Press, 1961), pp. 64–68.

12. See Thomas C. Schelling, *The Strategy of Conflict* (Cambridge: Harvard University Press, 1960), pp. 257–58.

13. It may be (and was) argued that the nature and location of the target of nuclear weapons would constitute usable limits on their employment. The point here is that use of yields within a somewhat artificial category called "tactical" was impractical as a signaling device because of the lack of distinguishing "boundaries" inherent in the weapons.

14. Good discussions of the political utility of nuclear weapons would include Bernard Brodie, *War and Politics* (New York: Macmillan Co., 1973), chap. 9; and Schelling, *The Strategy of Conflict*, pp. 74–77, and Appendix A.

4

NATO's Environment
and the Integration of
Tactical Nuclear Weapons

In the previous chapter on the development of the NATO alliance, the bipolar structure of the international political system reflected its distribution of economic, military, and political power. The United States and the Soviet Union, as the dominant actors within their respective groups, sought to consolidate power within their spheres and vis-à-vis one another. The United States, long a practitioner of isolation and wary of entanglement in the political affairs of Europe, gradually rejected that tradition of non-involvement and increasingly plunged into the leading role among the Western powers and, indeed, the world.

In seeking to counter the efforts of the Soviet Union to dominate the "rimland" of Western Europe, America took the lead in aiding the reconstruction of the economies of Europe and in developing Western trade, and contributed the largest share of financial, manpower, and material support of the Western security alliance. In return, the United States had the dominant voice in policy formulation. Because the other nations were still suffering politically and economically from the debilitating effects of the war, they accepted the leadership of the United States.[1] However, as economic and political conditions in the states of Western Europe began to improve, mainly as a result of the earlier efforts of the United States and because of integrationist efforts taken by Europe, the members of the alliance were much less willing to accept uncritically the direction set by the United States. Gaining confidence from its increased economic capacity, Western Europe was increasingly prepared to question the United States on matters of NATO policy, especially as it related to the issue of nuclear weapons.

Not only was the United States forced to contend with more assertive alliance members, but the opponent of the alliance had become more formidable as well. The Soviet Union had also developed economically and militarily since the advent of tactical nuclear weapons to NATO. This increase in the capability of the major opponent to NATO was to trouble further the policy-making waters upon which the United States had previously sailed. It is these changing economic, political, and military conditions external to NATO that will now concern us. Specifically, what was the impact of these changes on the performance of NATO? Was the economic and political resurgence of NATO states able to be translated into political power within the decision-making structure of the alliance? Did the Soviet threat affect alliance unity?

THE CHANGED ECONOMIC CONDITIONS

In a postwar attempt to rebuild the economies of Europe as a politically strong front against Soviet expansion and to provide a market for American exports, the United States had undertaken a long-term and extensive program of international economic sponsorship and management. The European Economic Recovery Program (or Marshall Plan) provided for the overall reconstruction of the economies of Europe. As an aid plan in force from 1948 to 1952, the United States gave sixteen European states $17 billion.[2]

During this period, the only currency strong enough to meet the demand for international liquidity was the American dollar, for the strength of the American economy was unscathed by the war's bombs.[3] The fixed relationship of the dollar to gold ($35 an ounce as set during the Bretton Woods Conference) and, most importantly, the American commitment to convert dollars into gold made the description of the dollar "as good as gold" a truism.

Some said the dollar was better than gold: it was more flexible than gold, it drew interest, and it was desperately needed by European nations to buy crucial imports for their survival and reconstruction.[4]

However, the mere demand for American dollars was not sufficient to make them appear. To purchase American goods, Europeans had to use American dollars—dollars the Europeans did not have. The strength of the dollar and the demand for American goods caused the United States to incur huge balance of payment surpluses, thereby exacerbating the problem. To reverse this trend, the United States deliberately pursued economic policies designed to run counter to the natural flow of economic forces by incurring a balance of payments deficit. From 1947 until 1958 the United States encouraged a dollar outflow, and from 1950 on it ran a deficit which provided dollars to Western Europe's economic systems.[5] Additionally, the United States sought to manage the system of trade by correcting any imbalances in the system. It attempted to solve its balance of payments surplus problem by outright grants and foreign military expenditures. It absorbed a large volume of European goods while supporting the European Payments Union, an intra-European clearing system designed to ease the convertibility of European currencies while discriminating against the dollar.

The American economy prospered because of the dollar outflow which led to the purchase of American products and services. But by 1960, the international economic system and America's position within that system were in jeopardy.[6] Paradoxically, the system which underpinned the international monetary arrangements in the post-World War II era was a process which inevitably contained the seeds for its own destruction. That process was the constant flow of dollars from America. The monetary system was built upon international confidence in gold, which was based in turn upon confidence in the American dollar and upon America's readiness to convert dollars to gold. However, if the deficit caused by the large volume of dollar outflow became too large, and confidence in either America's readiness or ability to convert dollars into gold became suspect, the entire system would be jeopardized.

By 1958, the United States was no longer interested in running a balance of payments deficit. The economies of Europe had recovered much of their vitality and their balance of payments accounts and official reserves equaled those of the United States. American holdings in gold, having been used to provide the basis for the backing of foreign currencies, were reduced from $24.4 billion in 1948 to $19.5 billion at the end of 1959.[7] By 1960, the dollar holding of foreign states exceeded the gold reserves of the United States, thereby undermining confidence in the American dollar and American management of the system. The concerns became manifest when the United States experienced its first run of the dollar in November 1960. As a result of this and a subsequent run on the British pound, there emerged a perception that the American management of the system was inadequate and the system itself would need to be supplemented. Subsequently, two management groups were formed. The first, called the Group of Ten, was formed in December 1961, to lend financial support to the International Monetary Fund to aid that institution in combating excessive currency speculation by private investors. The group also served as a forum for discussions and exchange of information on proposals for monetary reform—reform of the American-conceived and American-dominated system. An additional group, composed of the officials of the central banks of Europe and America, exchanged information about national policies affecting the international monetary system, and in time of financial crisis supported various currencies. It agreed in 1961 to form a "gold pool" to buy gold when it fell below $35 an ounce and to sell it when it rose above that limit. The formation of these groups does not mean that there was a collapse of the American dollar in the American economy, or in the leadership position of the United States. Rather, it merely reflected the fact that economic conditions in Europe had changed dramatically in the past decade.

America's once-dominant role within the international economic system was being challenged by a united Europe—not for that position of dominance, but rather for a position as an equal partner with proposals that ought to carry equal weight in the economic councils. This challenge was made possible in part by the efforts of the United States as described above, and in part by the integrationist policies pursued by the nations in Europe. Taking their cue from the military success of the NATO alliance, and building upon previous economic cooperation in the immediate postwar period, the states of Continental Europe undertook further economic integration.

Drawing upon the earlier success of the European Coal and Steel Community, several European states established the European Economic Community (EEC) in 1958.[8] Popularly known as the Common Market, its overall goal was to bind the members more tightly into an economic union. The benefits of such a union would be the elimination of tariffs and quotas between members, and abolition of restrictions on the intramember movement of labor, capital, and services, and a more favorable bargaining position vis-à-vis non-members, notably the United States. This changed nature of economic relations between a united, economically strong Europe and the United States was dramatized by the so-called Kennedy Round of General Agreements on Tariffs and Trade (GATT). During these negotiations for the mutual reduction of tariffs between the two trading partners, it was clear that the bargaining was between equals, and that there were major points of divergence about which the EEC was not prepared to compromise.[9] By pooling their resources, the countries of the Common Market were thus able to assert themselves economically and compete more favorably against the United States—with obvious attendant benefits.

PSYCHOLOGICAL CHANGE

Economic development via the Common Market was not the only basis for a challenge to the American hegemony. Desiring to be free psychologically from the aegis of America, France took the lead to deny Common Market membership to Great Britain in 1963. It did so because, to France, Britain's membership represented an attempt at continued domination by the Anglo/American consortium.[10] France, and to a lesser extent the other members of the EEC, was quite willing to forego the benefit of Great Britain's membership in order to rid itself of the yoke of American domination, for it was through London that Washington would exert its influence. It was France's contention that by banding together the states of the Common Market could more effectively resist pressure by the United States—pressure that had been successfully exerted for the previous twenty years. Although not universally shared initially, France's position on reducing the dominance of the United States increasingly gained favor within the EEC. The American reaction was not unexpected. Because of this reluctance to continue to suffer the domination of the United States, the Common Market was accused of being "inward looking" and not having the best interests of the West (i.e., the United States) at heart.

This arrangement of economic power and consequent reluctance to continue to acquiesce to the unquestioned leadership of the United States was also reflected in other international changes. Because of their weakened economic and political condition following the war, states of Western Europe were not able to continue effective rule over their colonial possessions. This condition, coupled with persistent U.S. demands for "self-determination of all peoples" and the concomitant rise of nationalism within the various colonial nations, produced a veritable explosion of new states in the early 1960s. Particularly in Africa, new states blossomed as the remaining European empires crumbled. By 1960, all the major empires of the states of Europe (France, Britain, Belgium, the Netherlands, and Italy—Portugal did not succumb until the 1970s) had been dismantled. This decline in the former colonial empires reduced those states' concern in world affairs from a global to a regional perspective, and further strengthened the appeal of Gaullism. Capitalizing on this narrowed perspective, France attempted to persuade these states to form a "Third Force of Europe," interposing itself as a major actor between the United States and the Soviet Union. Although this movement was not nearly as successful as France had hoped, it was made possible in part due to the nascent nationalism of the European states and in part due to the increasing danger inherent in a U.S./U.S.S.R. confrontation, a topic to which we shall now turn.

THE CHANGING SOVIET THREAT

This desire for more independence in the conduct of individual foreign policies was made possible by the favorable change in the economic conditions in Europe, the decolonization movement, and perhaps most importantly, by the changed military environment of the NATO alliance. Since the end of World War II, the Soviet Union had maintained a military establishment composed primarily of land forces which were concerned with occupation duty in the satellite countries of Eastern Europe. While these land forces were sufficiently large to pose a threat to Western Europe, the Soviet Union did not possess the capability to project its military power beyond the land mass of Eurasia. Unlike the United States, the Soviet Union possessed only a minimal air force designed primarily for air defense and a small navy for coastal patrolling. In short, it had neither the fleet of bomber aircraft nor capital ships to allow it to project its military capability overseas. The stirrings of change to this military capability began in 1949. In August of that year, the Soviet Union exploded its first atomic bomb approximately five years ahead of Western intelligence estimates.[11] In 1953, again ahead of intelligence estimates, the Soviet Union exploded the more powerful hydrogen bomb.

The most stunning example of the increase in Soviet military capability, however, was the dramatic launching of the world's first satellite into space in 1957. This feat demonstrated clearly that the Soviet Union had, or would soon have, the capability to strike either Western Europe or the continental United States with nuclear weapons, using intercontinental missiles. Therefore, this was a fundamental change in the perceived balance of military power between these two blocs of states and one which was to have serious consequences for the NATO alliance.

Prior to 1957 the NATO alliance had relied upon the tactical and strategic nuclear weapons of the United States to provide the substitute for manpower to deter its wars. It was reasoned that the nuclear capability of the United States would ensure that no state would be tempted to test the mettle of the alliance, for certain destruction of the aggressor would be the result. This concept for deterrence of war was predicated on the possession of an overwhelming military capability by the alliance. Once the asymmetry of that capability was questioned, as it was after the Soviet space achievements of 1957, then the strategy itself came under increasingly heavy attack. And as the strategy for NATO defense came into question, other strains in the alliance were revealed. These strains were in part symptomatic of the times, as discussed above, and in part of a function of the manner in which tactical nuclear weapons had been integrated into the alliance. It is this manner of integration of the tactical nuclear weapons into the NATO alliance that will now be discussed.

NEW TECHNOLOGY ACCEPTANCE

America's tactical nuclear weapons were never truly integrated into the NATO military force structures. Although America professed to provide the tactical nuclear weapons to the alliance, this was not the case in reality. The United States had dispatched to Europe "several thousand" tactical nuclear weapons as the means whereby the alliance could "beef up its punch."[12] As the ultimate military guarantor of the alliance, the United States was to provide these weapons and employ them in accordance with the treaty's provisions—that is, on request of the alliance itself and by consent of the American president. But since the United States was the first member of develop this new technology, and since its high cost prohibited other alliance members from acquiring it unilaterally, the United States alone possessed, and thereby controlled, the employment of these weapons.

Its control of these weapons was not only political, but physical as well. Naturally enough, the nuclear weapons developed by the United States were designed to be employed by American armaments. American nuclear artillery shells were manufactured in the same caliber as American artillery pieces. American nuclear bombs were manufactured to be hung on the bomb racks of American aircraft. Since the designs of artillery pieces and bomb racks were not standardized within NATO, American nuclear weapons "fit" only American military hardware, thereby further ensuring American control within NATO.[13]

The sole control of nuclear weapons by the United States was not initially perceived by the alliance to be a matter of concern. If nuclear weapons were, as President Eisenhower said, the same as a bullet, then no special precautions or procedures needed to be developed to govern their use.[14] Consequently, there were none. The doctrine for employment of nuclear weapons had progressed no further than the rather vague notion that they would be employed "when needed." The specifics of under what circumstances might the use of nuclear weapons be authorized; the number, type, and yield; and the location and nature of the type of targets to be attacked, were never addressed.[15] Rather, the principle of unanimity of action prevailed. If one member objected to a proposed course of action by the alliance, that action was not binding on the objector.[16] In principle, then, the United States, as the sole possessor of nuclear weapons within NATO, might frustrate the desires of the other members of the alliance. It could refuse to employ them when requested, or as the physical controller of these weapons it could employ them even if not so requested by the alliance. Either condition was troubling to the other members of the alliance. But, despite their growing economic and political powers, European members of NATO were unable to translate those capabilities into effective leverage within the alliance.

By the early 1960s, despite American protestations of harmony with the desires of the alliance, there developed the suspicion that the United States "doth protest too much." It was the Cuban Missile Crisis that crystallized the dilemma of NATO. The United States, troubled that the introduction of missiles into Cuba would fundamentally and drastically alter the balance of military power with the Soviet Union and that such a blatant challenge to American security could not go unmet, threatened nuclear war if the missiles were not removed. The Soviet Union, fearing that war, removed the missiles. For the Allies, the results of that confrontation and subsequent efforts by the two dominant powers to reduce tensions were prophetic. European nations reached the conclusion that neither of the two main nuclear powers desired to risk military confrontation with each other even when their individual vital interests were at stake. Their desire to risk war on behalf of an ally was deemed even more problematical.

Conciliatory efforts by the United States and the Soviet Union, such as the Hotline Agreement and the Partial Test Ban Treaty portended to Europe an era of reduced tensions. It may seem incongruous that Europeans were at the same time troubled by a dramatic increase in Soviet strategic power and by the apparent reduced likelihood of a confrontation between the Soviets and the principal alliance member. However, this curious phenomenon was the case and, coupled with the other changes within the environment and within the alliance, was to produce serious strains upon the cohesion and efficacy of NATO. The focus of the problems of the alliance centered around the employment of tactical nuclear weapons and their relation to the changed nature of the environment and the status of the members of the alliance. It is at this point that a net assessment of the effect of tactical nuclear weapons on the alliance can now be made.

NOTES

1. In discussing the circumstances under which Europe accepted American leadership, President de Gaulle of France recalled: "Thus it never happened that a government belonging to NATO took an attitude that diverged from that of the White House." While obviously an overstatement of the relations within the alliance, it nonetheless characterizes the American dominance. Charles de Gaulle, *Memoirs of Hope: Renewal and Endeavor*, trans. Terence Kilmartin (New York: Simon and Schuster, 1971), p. 200.

2. Henry T. Nash, *American Foreign Policy*, rev. ed. (Homewood, IL: Dorsey Press, 1978), pp. 42-43.

3. This section on monetary activities is taken from Joan Edelman Spero, *The Politics of International Economic Relations* (New York: St. Martin's Press, 1977), chap. 2.

4. Ibid., p. 36.

5. Ibid.

6. Ibid., pp. 37-43.

7. Ibid., p. 38.

8. The section on the EEC is taken from John W. Spanier, *American Foreign Policy Since World War II*, 9th ed. (New York: Holt, Rinehart and Winston, 1983), p. 93; and Spero, *Politics of International Economic Relations*, chap. 3.

9. Spero, *Politics of International Economic Relations*, pp. 77-78.

10. The Benelux countries, Germany, and Italy tended to see merit in continued negotiations to bring Great Britain into the Common Market, although they too were concerned about the special considerations that Great Britain attached to its membership. The de Gaulle government strongly opposed the incorporation of Great Britain and the other members were content to let France lead the drive to deny the British, and

thus let it "take the heat." It was only after the demise of the de Gaulle regime and a perceived reorientation of Great Britain "toward the Continent" that its bid was accepted ten years later. See J. Warren Nystrom and George W. Hoffman, *The Common Market* (New York: D. Van Nostrand Co., 1976), pp. 20-23.

11. Samuel P. Huntington, *The Common Defense* (New York: Columbia University Press, 1961), p. 47.

12. Ibid., p. 74.

13. Currently, many NATO members possess military equipment manufactured by the United States and, hence, could conceivably use that equipment to launch U.S.-made nuclear weapons. but such was not the case in the 1950s. Equipment of European armies was almost exclusively of European manufacture and not compatible with U.S. equipment.

14. *New York Times*, 17 March 1955, p. 1.

15. Indeed, critics of America's current defense policy argue that no clear policy for NATO's employment of tactical nuclear weapons exists even today. See William R. Van Cleave and S. T. Cohen, *Tactical Nuclear Weapons: An Examination of the Issues* (New York: Crane, Russak and Company, Inc., 1978), pp. 54-63.

16. Edwin H. Fedder, *NATO: The Dynamics of Alliance in the Post-War World* (New York: Dodd, Mead and Co., 1973), chap. 4.

5

Tactical Nuclear Weapons— An Assessment

The illusion of the 1940s that NATO was to operate as a partnership of equal members was by the 1960s clearly shown to be just that. By virtue of its superior military capability, its wartime legacy, its carefully guarded nuclear monopoly, and its status as the ultimate guarantor of the alliance, the United States immediately assumed the dominant position within a NATO desperately in need of American power. Offering the use, but not the control, of its tactical nuclear weapons as a substitute for expensive manpower, the United States maintained the military capability of the alliance in the face of European force reductions, and thereby reduced alliance strains. It also continued its dominance.

By the early 1960s, the environment of the alliance had changed. Western Europe had recovered a major portion of its economic and political health and had become increasingly dissatisfied with America's style of leadership. Militarily, the Soviet Union had dramatically demonstrated its missile-born capability to deliver nuclear weapons, and cries of a "missile gap" demonstrated Western concern. The Soviet-American confrontation over the presence of missiles in Cuba and the resultant impetus to seek ways to avoid further crises ushered in an era of reduced tensions and seemed to demonstrate that both sides now considered nuclear war unthinkable. It was this apparent revulsion at the idea of nuclear war and the relation of that idea to NATO strategy for defense which were to cause the quiescent strains in the alliance to be exposed to all who would see them.[1] While there had always existed some debate concerning the details of the alliance's strategy, that debate was generally over the "fine points" and engaged in only by the professional military. The issue raised subsequent to the introduction of tactical nuclear weapons, however, were more serious and more widely debated.

THE ISSUE OF STRATEGY—THE INITIAL ROUND

The starting point for the debate on the proper strategy for the integration and employment of nuclear weapons by NATO is somewhat easy to discern; the various directions and branches of it after a few years are less so. The initial debate was fairly muted. It was joined shortly after the announcement in 1954 of the intention of NATO to incorporate tactical nuclear weapons into its arsenal as a substitute for manpower. In principle, it was considered cheaper to rely on the firepower of tactical nuclear weapons to achieve what had formerly been required of manpower. The debate over the validity of this proposition was slow to develop and centered around the assumption that nuclear war would require fewer people to fight it. Proponents of the "firepower for manpower" substitution argued for a direct trade-off: nuclear weapons make large numbers of conventional forces unnecessary.[2]

Opponents in the debate retorted that troops would still be necessary to fire those weapons and regain lost territory, and that the increased degree of destruction and personnel casualties would require more—not fewer—troops to fight the battle. Replacements of men and equipment would be required for the combat casualties and more support personnel would be required to treat the wounded, move the supplies, and so forth.[3] Almost as a secondary issue, the contribution of tactical nuclear weapons to the deterrent strategy of the alliance was mentioned. Just as the threat of America's strategic nuclear weapons was to deter Communist aggression in the peripheral areas, so too, would tactical nuclear weapons increase the deterrent effect of the alliance. Since in 1954 the Soviets did not possess tactical nuclear weapons in any quantity and the threat of America's strategic arsenal was so great, not much thought was given to the prospect of fighting with tactical nuclear weapons. In great measure, this initial debate was still-born, since the members of NATO gladly accepted the less expensive nuclear option. They subsequently reduced the size of their military establishments and professed reliance on both tactical nuclear weapons and America's strategic nuclear arms.

THE STRATEGY—WHAT TO DO WITH WHAT KIND OF FORCES?

The debate on overall strategy was revived in the late 1950s by two factors: the Sputnik-demonstrated increase in Soviet strategic capability which now clearly threatened the continental United States with nuclear weapons, and the resurgence of Europe's economic and political health and the resultant demand for a more equal share in decision-making power with the United States. The particular strand of the debate over NATO strategy to which one adhered was in great measure dependent upon the implications one drew from the above conditions and from one's assessment of the ability of combatants to exercise and communicate restraint in war. There were six more or less distinct groups of thinkers on NATO strategy, and the membership of each was not static.

The first group might be called "Conventional War Strategists."[4] This group was fearful of the possibility that the initial use of tactical nuclear weapons in Europe would escalate to the level of a strategic exchange between the United States and the Soviet Union, resulting in the virtual destruction of those societies. Consequently, reliance on nuclear weapons was inadvisable and, instead, the conventional forces of NATO should be developed so that resort to tactical nuclear weapons would not be required. For this group, the link between combat in Europe and reliance on the American strategic capability was not desirable, for it irrevocably tied war in Europe to war in America. Not surprisingly, the membership of this group was predominantly American.

Another group with perhaps a more sanguine view of the inevitability of escalation might be called the "Limited War Strategists."[5] This group viewed tactical nuclear weapons as instruments of policy, relying more on their communication potential than their military effects to achieve desired goals. To this group, military weapons served a much larger purpose than their destructive capacity. They were to be employed as signals of determination or restraint. As such, the group rejected the inevitability of escalation to strategic nuclear warfare and substituted instead a greater faith in the ability of policy makers to control events in wartime. For this group, tactical nuclear weapons would be a necessary substitute for conventional forces since alliance members could not provide those forces. Tactical nuclear weapons were to be used in a discriminating manner to defeat the enemy with a minimum of destruction or to convince him of the futility of his efforts. The linkage of battlefield nuclear weapons to America's strategic means should be maintained and, indeed, exhibited as a threat of additional military power that could be brought to bear. However, the precise nature of that linkage should not be revealed in order to assure flexibility to policy makers.

Two less widely supported positions on NATO strategy were those that questioned the need and utility of the alliance. One position held that with the advent of nuclear weapons by the Soviet Union/Warsaw Pact, the alliance itself was rendered useless, and therefore its strategy was unimportant.[6] The initial use of nuclear weapons by either side would require the opponent's response and escalation to strategic weapons would occur, resulting in the destruction of both sides. Since no state would be willing to risk its survival for the defense of another, military alliances would not exist in the nuclear age. Hence, it was idle to speak of a NATO strategy.

The other group which questioned the need for the alliance also foresaw warfare's inevitable escalation to strategic nuclear war and the resulting implications for the entire world. The solution was not to determine the optimum military strategy, but for all states to disarm themselves and seek peace through the cultivation of the natural community of interests of man.[7] Here, too, neither alliance nor strategy was necessary. As fear of arms races, missile gaps, and the number of air raid bomb shelters and civil defense programs grew, so did support for disarmament, albeit still at a modest level. With the aftermath of the Cuban Missile Crisis and the gradual lessening of tensions between the United States and the Soviet Union, this stand on NATO strategy and the alliance itself largely disappeared from the professional journals. Recently, however, it shows signs of rebirth, especially in the left wing of the British Labour Party and the Green Movement on the Continent.

The final two predominant strands of the debate which were to evolve are still with us today and are the basis for continued strain within the alliance. As with other strands of debate, the first group viewed the direct relationship between tactical nuclear weapons and America's strategic means with concern.[8] NATO's reliance on tactical nuclear weapons in lieu of a conventional war-fighting capability precluded a defense using conventional forces and forced early resort to the use of tactical nuclear weapons, which, in turn, would likely escalate to the employment of strategic nuclear weapons. Given the immense destruction inherent in the use of strategic nuclear weapons, this was a course of action to be avoided, yet was seen as the only alternative to capitulation. Reduction of conventional forces to low levels of capability not only precluded a conventional defense of Europe, but such a weakened status invited the very attack that was to be deterred. Rather than be forced either to rely only on nuclear weapons, with the attendant high probability of suffering severe destruction in Europe and the United States, or capitulate without much of a fight, NATO required a more flexible strategy.[9]

Conventional forces were needed in strength to deter an initial attack, and failing that, to preclude the necessity of early resort to the use of tactical nuclear weapons by providing the capability for a defense using conventional weapons. But tactical nuclear weapons were still required to reinforce the deterrent effect of the conventional forces, to provide a deterrent to the enemy's use of tactical nuclear weapons, and, should that deterrent effort fail, to provide a war-fighting capability to bolster that of the conventional forces.

The linkage of NATO's tactical nuclear weapons to America's strategic deterrent was still present in this concept, but to its opponents, this strategy as a means of defending Europe was increasingly suspect. Given the flexibility inherent in such a war-fighting strategy, America now seemed to have a range of choices to decide at what level of European hostilities it would employ its strategic capability. It seemed that under this concept of NATO strategy, the familiar roles of the sword and shield had been reversed. Rather than conventional/tactical nuclear forces being the shield which blunted the attack while the American strategic sword devastated the Soviet homeland, the American strategic capability was now the shield which was to prevent escalation of the battle to intercontinental strategic nuclear warfare while NATO's sword of conventional/tactical nuclear forces defeated the enemy. It was the "flexibility" of this new proposed strategy that was troubling to the final group of proponents of a new NATO strategy.

For this group, the flexibility to be brought about by the proposed increase in conventional forces was a dangerous weakening of the deterrent capacity of the alliance.[10] By providing "options" on how (and, they wondered sotto voce, "if") America's guarantee to defend NATO with its strategic nuclear capability was to operate, the credibility of that guarantee was immediately suspect. Rather, one should remove all doubt about the guarantee by downplaying the element of choice—the linkage between war in Europe and America's strategic means should be firm and immediate. To allow America the luxury of deciding the circumstances under which it would strike the Soviet heartland and, hence, invite retaliation and destruction would effectively allow America to decide the fate of Western Europe. Indeed, one of the more apocalyptic visions hypothesized:

Who can say that if the occasion arises the two [the Soviet Union and the United States], while each deciding not to launch its missiles at the main enemy [each other], so that itself should be spared, will not crush the others? It is possible to imagine that on some awful day Western Europe should be wiped out from Moscow and Central Europe from Washington.[11]

Proponents of this version of NATO's strategy saw the notion of "flexibility" as an opportunity for abdication of strategic responsibility by America, which might well invite a testing of that guarantee. Therefore, efforts to increase conventional force capabilities would actually be detrimental to the deterrent capability of the alliance. Tactical nuclear weapons should be an integral part of

NATO defenses and there should be no doubt of their use, or of their linkage to America's strategic means, according to this strand of thought.

Such debates were obscurants for the more fundamental political problems of NATO. In reality, the problems concerned the status of the members as equal decision-making partners in the alliance, especially as related to the use of nuclear weapons, and, hence their survival. If NATO was ever "marketed on an illusion" that the alliance "would lead to a true partnership of equals with virtually identical interests," that illusion was surely being tested in the early 1960s.[12] The increasing economic and political health of the European members of the alliance, and the loss of their former colonial empires were strong inducements toward Europe's efforts at redressing the balance of political power within NATO. Just as strongly, the United States was to resist those demands and retain control over the tactical nuclear weapons within Europe. The tug of war for nuclear decision-making power in the alliance had a centrifugal effect on the alliance and the manner in which the United States attempted to respond to this strain is the final area for consideration.

RESPONSE TO THE PROBLEM OF DECISION MAKING

The postwar recovery by the members of NATO and the yearning for a more equal voice in policy formulation was no more evident than with France. For centuries, a great power with vast overseas holdings throughout the world, France had a proud history of substantial influence in international affairs. But the debilitation of World War I, the rapid collapse of French forces during World War II, and the shattered economy thereafter had forced France to accept the economic, military and, hence, political dominance of the United States.[13] These circumstances were a great blow to a French psyche more accustomed to a greater degree of influence in world affairs.[14] In time, the French state regained its economic health via the Marshall Plan and European efforts at economic integration while it accepted the military security afforded by NATO. By the early 1960s, France had sufficiently recovered to contemplate credibly its intention to withdraw its forces from NATO and pursue a more independent foreign policy. A primary impetus for this maneuver lay in the decision-making control over the employment of nuclear weapons in support of a battle in Europe.[15]

France, intent on symbolizing European concerns, wanted to ensure that the decision to resort to tactical and then strategic weapons in support of a European battle was a non-decision—that is, it was to be an automatic response to be taken early in the battle. Fearing this frightful eventuality, the initial attack by the Soviet Union would be deterred. The French viewed American attempts to obtain "flexibility" as damaging to the American strategic guarantee and, in effect, placing French and European survival at the whim of Washington. To preclude this unacceptable status, to shore up deterrence by making the linkage to America's strategic means less "flexible" and thereby to regain a voice in its own survival, and to project a more powerful leadership image to the rest of Europe, France elected to pursue its own strategic nuclear arms program. Called the *force de frappe*, this initially-modest nuclear capability was designed to place France's finger on America's nuclear trigger.[16] By possessing its own nuclear forces, France could also dictate the circumstances under which nuclear weapons, and presumably escalation to America's strategic means, would be employed. To underscore its determination to regain a greater measure of foreign policy control, France withdrew militarily from NATO in 1966 and evicted all NATO staffs and facilities from its territory.

In an attempt to defuse the controversy of decision-making authority in the employment of nuclear weapons in NATO, the United States made several efforts at devising a satisfactory means for increasing the status of the other members and sharing that decision-making power, yet not relinquishing control of its nuclear weapons. The initial effort to establish a Multi-Lateral Force (MLF) was proposed as a "hardware" solution to what was a political problem.[17] The primary objectives of America in the creation of the MLF were threefold: to assuage European concerns about the willingness of America to use strategic nuclear weapons, and hence risk American cities in the defense of Europe, to create the appearance of a more equitable distribution of decision-making power within the alliance, and as a compelling rationale for other states (notably France, Great Britain, and West Germany) not to pursue their own independent nuclear force.[18] The MLF was to be a naval force assigned to NATO for employment by the military command of NATO. Its precise composition underwent many iterations, from American missile-firing submarines assigned to NATO with and without mixed-manned crews, to multination surface ships with nuclear missiles, to surface ships with mixed-manned crews. In each version of the MLF concept, however, the authority to release the nuclear weapons for operational employment to NATO continued to reside with the American president.

For Europe, the lessons of the series of American proposals on the MLF were both painful and clear. First, the pivotal issue in any strategy on the employment of nuclear weapons was the initial decision to release those weapons for employment. Second, the United States was convinced that the employment of strategic nuclear weapons against the Soviet homeland posed grave risks for America and therefore, lastly, the United States was not prepared to allow willingly that decision-making capacity to reside with anyone except the president.

As it became clear that the MLF would not preclude either Great Britain or France from the development of its own national strategic forces, and as the requirements for tight control over the employment of nuclear weapons inherent in the strategy of "flexible response" became clear, interest in the MLF in Europe and America waned and the idea gradually faded from governmental view by 1965.

Other efforts were similarly counterproductive. Under United States sponsorship, a high-level planning committee was created to coordinate the strategy for employment of tactical nuclear weapons. The Nuclear Defense Affairs Committee and the Nuclear Planning Group were created ostensibly to increase member participation in nuclear planning, and hence, release of nuclear weapons.[19] However, this structural change to the alliance was only cosmetic. Since each member retained veto power over any substantive proposal by these committees, American control over nuclear weapons was retained. It could veto any request for release of tactical nuclear weapons. The other, perhaps more draconian, side of the coin was that as the physical possessor of the tactical nuclear weapons, the United States could unilaterally employ the weapons without the consent of NATO. Control was therefore complete. The United States could employ tactical nuclear weapons if it suited its interests, or not do so if it did not. This was the best of all possible "flexible" worlds, at least for the United States.

The American attempts to soothe the European worries over the validity of its strategic guarantee and to provide increased status to NATO states as members or pseudo-members of the exclusive "nuclear club" were, therefore, counterproductive. That at once the United States was unwilling to relinquish full control over the MLF to NATO, that it argued against the pursuit of independent strategic nuclear forces by other NATO members, and that it could veto any nuclear-related matter only enhanced what European members had already suspected: the American strategic guarantee was not as ironclad as it was once touted to be, nuclear weapons were the basis for political as well as military power, and America would not willingly share true decision-making authority within NATO, thereby reinforcing the European position as the junior member of the firm.

Faced with these conclusions, the French continued the withdrawal of their military forces from the alliance, other members devoted a decreasing portion of their gross national product toward defense, and reduced the social costs of military service by either decreasing the number of their youth in uniform or the duration of their service, or both.[20] For its part, the United States wrung its hands and decried the lack of support by its allies, called for increased "burden sharing" by them, and actively pursued a policy to make its options flexible—a flexibility which Europe suspected as the capacity to desert it in its hour of greatest need. But it steadfastly refused to devolve any control of its nuclear weapons to its allies and instead pursued a policy of non-proliferation of nuclear weapons which would effectively deny other states from having a nuclear capability.

TACTICAL NUCLEAR WEAPONS—THE RESULT

If the frequency and intensity of the bickering between members, a declining membership, and a declining commitment of resources devoted to the military and NATO are valid indicators, the level of cohesion and efficacy of the alliance was decreasing from that of its earlier years. To be sure, events outside the alliance had certainly served to alter the conditions under which it was founded, as did the individual policies which its individual members pursued. But NATO, without a full appreciation of its political effects, had embraced the technology of tactical nuclear weapons as the military linchpin of the alliance. The result, as its political effects became more clearly understood, became debilitating to the alliance, producing the opposite condition.

In summary, the adoption of tactical nuclear weapons allowed members to decrease their resources devoted to NATO with less of a feeling of risk, and thereby forced them to fight a nuclear war, should war come. This risk was accepted, initially, because of economic benefits which outweighed the military costs, and the existence of the American nuclear guarantee. As the technology spread to the Soviet Union and its military capability increased, that guarantee became suspect and the prospect of having to fight with nuclear weapons became increasingly unattractive. Disunity within the alliance mounted as increasingly restive members debated the proper strategy for the use of tactical nuclear weapons, the proper governing procedures for their release, and the role of conventional forces in a nuclear environment. As the sole authority for release of its nuclear weapons, the United States refused to devolve meaningfully that authority within any NATO governing structure and continued to provide a strategic guarantee which was increasingly drained of its credibility. But with that promise, the United States could continue to exercise a sometimes tenuous but nonetheless real military control over Europe—a control it was rapidly losing in the economic sphere.

NATO Europe, although fearing America's declining credibility, was equally desirous of receiving that pledge. For Europe, the function of tactical nuclear weapons as a link to the larger umbrella of strategic nuclear weapons was the process which allowed it not to develop its conventional war capability with low risk and at great economic and social savings. It was content to suffer occasional (and increasingly less frequent and severe) American military heavy-handedness for those benefits. Tactical nuclear weapons, although they initially seemed to solve alliance problems, had longer term, generally deleterious consequences for the environment, alliance governing structures, force levels, strategy, and hence alliance unity.

NOTES

1. For its part, the United States officially refused to acknowledge the changed circumstances of the alliance. It proclaimed its good faith to Europe and pledged its strategic weapons, but refused to recognize that the Soviet buildup had drained the credibility from that promise.

2. Secretary of Defense Charles E. Wilson testified before Congress that ground forces armed with tactical nuclear weapons could be less numerous than those without. U.S. Congress, Senate, Committee on Appropriations, *Department of Defense Appropriations*. 83d Cong., 2nd sess., 1954, p. 8.

3. James E. King, Jr., "Nuclear Plenty and Limited War," *Foreign Affairs* 35 (January 1957): 245.

4. A sample of the writings of the proponents of the necessity for a greater conventional war capability would be Ferdinand O. Miksche, "Is the Atomic Deterrent a Bluff?," in *The Military-Technical Revolution*, ed. John Erickson (New York: Praeger Publishers, 1966), p. 35; James E. King, Jr., "Collective Defense: The Military Commitment," in *Alliance Policy in the Cold War*, ed. Arnold Wolfers (Baltimore: Johns Hopkins University Press, 1959), p. 103; Thomas C. Schelling, *The Strategy of Conflict* (Cambridge; Harvard University Press, 1960); John Strachey, *On the Prevention of War* (New York: St. Martin's Press, 1963); Richard N. Rosecrance, "Can We Limit Nuclear War?," *Military Review* 38 (March 1959): 51; Paul H. Nitze, "Atoms, Strategy and Policy," *Foreign Affairs* 34 (January 1956): 187; and B. H. Liddell Hart, *Deterrent or Defense* (New York: Praeger Publishers, 1960).

5. Perhaps the most notable example of the limited war concept was Henry A. Kissinger, *Nuclear Weapons and Foreign Policy* (New York: Harper Brothers, 1957). Although he later changed his position on the desirability of the use of tactical weapons to fight a limited war in Europe, Kissinger's work was nonetheless prominent. See also Bernard Brodie, *Strategy in the Missile Age* (Princeton: Princeton University Press, 1959).

6. See, for example, Pierre M. Gallois, "U.S. Strategy and the Defense of the Europe," *Orbis* 7 (Summer 1963): 226. This viewpoint reflected what was to become the basis for French foreign policy.

7. The most well-known proponent of disarmament in this period was Bertrand Russell. See Bertrand Russell, *Common Sense and Nuclear Warfare* (New York: Simon and Schuster, 1959).

8. Leading proponents of this position in the debate over NATO's nuclear strategy were Henry A. Kissinger, "Limited War: Conventional or Nuclear?," in *Arms Control, Disarmament, and National Security*, ed. Donald G. Brennan (New York: George Braziller, 1961), p. 138, and Maxwell D. Taylor, *The Uncertain Trumpet* (New York: Harper Brothers, 1959). As noted above, Kissinger's position is a change from his previous view of the consequences of escalation from limited war with tactical nuclear weapons to strategic nuclear war.

9. This strategy was adopted initially by the Kennedy administration in 1961. Later, with some significant modifications to the role to be played by conventional forces, it was adopted in 1967 as NATO policy. See Alain C. Enthoven and K. Wayne Smith, *How Much is Enough?* (New York: Harper and Row, 1971; Harper Colophon, 1972), chap. 4.

10. This position in the strategy debate was one held primarily by Europeans. See Helmut Schmidt, *Defense or Retaliation: A German View* (New York: Praeger Publishers, 1962); Paul-Henri Spaak, "The Atom Bomb and NATO," *Foreign Affairs* 33 (April 1955): 335; Andre Beufre, *NATO and Europe*, trans. Joseph Green (New York: Vintage Books, 1966); Glenn H. Snyder, *Deterrence and Defense* (Princeton: Princeton University Press, 1961); Hellmuth Roth, "The Organizational Crisis in NATO," in *The Military-Technical Revolution*, ed. John Erickson (New York: Praeger Publishers, 1966), p. 116.

11. "Press Conference of the President of France," *New York Times*, 11 November 1962, cited by Seyom Brown, *The Faces of Power: Constancy and Change in U.S. Foreign Policy from Truman to Johnson* (New York: Columbia University Press, 1969), p. 184.

12. Paraphrased from Ronald Steel, "The Abdication of Europe," *The New Republic* 1 May 1976, p. 14.

13. While somewhat overstated, the comment of President de Gaulle captured the anguish of France: "Once the declaration of principle known as the Atlantic Alliance had been adopted in Washington, the North Atlantic Treaty Organization had been set up, under the terms of which our defense and hence our foreign policy disappeared into a system directed from abroad, while an American generalissimo with headquarters near Versailles exercised over the old world the military authority of the new."

Charles de Gaulle, *Memoirs of Hope: Renewal and Endeavor*, trans. Terence Kilmartin (New York: Simon and Schuster, 1971), p. 11.

14. Again, de Gaulle reflects on the necessity of a more unfettered French foreign policy: "The French people had for centuries grown accustomed to think of their country as the Mastodon of Europe. . . . Now once again circumstances . . . offer them the chance of fulfilling an international mission without which they would lose interest in themselves and fall into disruption." De Gaulle, *Memoirs of Hope*, p. 178.

15. De Gaulle, *Memoirs of Hope*, pp. 200-204. While the problem of control over the tactical nuclear weapons assigned to NATO was real, the larger problem for France and for Europe was the reliability of America as the strategic guarantor. Even if the problem of the decision to employ tactical nuclear weapons could have been solved, there remained the problem of the ultimate American guarantee, a problem which was to remain unsolved. For France in particular, there also remained the problem of reliance on a foreign state for its ultimate survival. For France, this was unacceptable.

16. Those nuclear weapons stored in Europe which are made available to certain NATO members are retained under American control by a so-called "two-key" system. Both keys are under American control and procedures require two persons to be present whenever access to nuclear weapons is necessary. After receipt of proper authority, U.S. custodial personnel will release the designated weapons to host countries for employment. At U.S. delivery sites in Europe, nuclear weapons are also under similar two-man control. Additionally, proper release authority must be received to employ these weapons. Without proper release authority, even without two-person control procedures, the weapons could not be functionally employed. A host country's objections to employment of American nuclear weapons from its soil may be a rather moot point, if U.S. forces are operating in that host country. Since release authority for nuclear weapons flows through U.S. as well as NATO operational channels, host country agreement to launch nuclear weapons from its soil is not required. The American president, however, has agreed to consult in this matter with host country leadership "time and circumstances permitting."

17. A most detailed account of the attempts at formulation of the Multi-Lateral Force (MLF) may be found in John D. Steinbruner, *The Cybernetic Theory of Decision* (Princeton: Princeton University Press, 1974). See also, Brown, *The Faces of Power*, pp. 179-81; Timothy W. Stanley, *NATO in Transition: The Future of the Atlantic Alliance* (New York: Praeger Publishers, 1965); and Henry A. Kissinger, *The Troubled Partnership* (Garden City, NY: Doubleday and Co., 1966).

18. As Steinbruner makes abundantly clear, both support for and opposition to the MLF among elements of the American government and the various states of Europe varied almost with the identity of the actor in the policy process. The objectives listed herein are from the Department of Defense and the Department of State.

19. U.S. Department of Defense, *The Theater Nuclear Force Posture in Europe*, by James R. Schlesinger, A Report to the U.S. Congress in compliance with Public Law 93-365 (Washington, DC: U.S. Government Printing Office, 1975), p. 26.

20. Robert E. Osgood, *NATO: The Entangling Alliance* (Chicago: University of Chicago Press, 1962), pp. 118-28; *also* Appendixes 1 and 2.

6

Centrifugal Forces in the 1960s

In 1959, as if discovering an eternal truth, scholars wrote of the "stresses and strains in 'going it with others.' "[1] The NATO alliance, which had been formed in war's aftermath as a deterrent to another, more costly war, had suffered its share of vicissitudes. Questions of equitable force goals, German rearmament, and extra-alliance adventures such as Suez had bedeviled the alliance during its first decade. But each time the Soviet Union had obliged to end at least temporarily the bickering by providing a crisis and resultant rallying point for the allies. Trouble in Hungary, Berlin, or bellicose talk of "letting the missiles fly," was usually sufficient to shift the attention of the alliance to an external threat. Because these crises only delayed but did not solve NATO's problems, it should not be surprising that at the end of the 1960s the alliance remained beset with problems. Many of those problems had their origin in the environment of the alliance.

The strains between the poles of the bipolar environment of the 1950s had been replaced by those within a multipolar world. New economic and technological forces had revamped the global distribution of power and resulted in the renewed political confidence of Western Europe. Nor was the Eastern bloc immune from these forces. The Soviet Union, in gaining a powerful nuclear capability, had become increasingly circumspect concerning its ulti-

mate use. Publicly, the People's Republic of China was less sanguine about the means to achieve a Communist triumph and an
acrimonious debate preceded the outright break in relations between members of the former Communist monolith. For its part,
the United States was preoccupied with the burden of fighting a
limited war in Southeast Asia and was growing reluctant to commit further forces abroad. Both factors contributed to the inability
of the United States to maintain a constant level of forces in Europe and threatened to reduce Europe's confidence in America's
pledges of support to NATO.

The alliance itself continued to grapple with the dilemma of
providing sufficient means to counteract its opponent's increasing
strength. The earlier promise of tactical nuclear weapons to provide a substitute for manpower had faded. Those weapons had
become instead a symbol of controversy between the United States
and the rest of the alliance. Feeling confined by what it viewed as
the previous "all or nothing" policy and fearing the effects of a
Soviet response to an American fulfillment of its strategic pledge
of support to NATO, the United States had pushed instead for a
NATO strategy which included "more options." After years of
reluctance, in 1967 NATO ratified a concept of "flexible response" for its defense, but remained convinced that American
efforts to implement it drained the credibility from its promise of
supreme military support for NATO.

It was roughly at this juncture that a new weapon technology
gained credence as a possible solution to NATO's military ills.
Relatively inexpensive, very accurate, and non-nuclear, precision-
guided munitions appeared to be able to provide cheaply firepower that was well below the "threshold" of nuclear weapons,
and allow the defeat of a superior Soviet force. The nature of this
new weapon technology and how it actually affected the NATO
alliance is the subject of this case study. As with tactical nuclear
weapons some two decades before, this new weapon technology
did not have a simple cause-and-effect relationship with the alliance. Its appearance was concurrent with other forces acting on
the alliance both from within and without; as such, its effect is
somewhat difficult to discern. However, by first examining some
of the forces affecting the alliance, one may gain some clarity.

As before, the focus of this case study will be on the United

States, the linchpin of the alliance. In terms of supplying military forces, monetary support, and the impetus of policy making, the United States had been the dominant actor within the alliance. However, this leadership role had been steadily diminishing during the past twenty years and was a source for controversy within the alliance. In part, the reasons for this decline in the status of the United States were due to changes in the structure and distribution of power within the environment of the alliance. The causes for these changes may be classed as economic, ideological, military, and psychological, and will serve as a basis for the initial discussion in the next case study.

This case study is divided into two major parts. The first part is "pre-technology" and will deal with the environment, the alliance, and the technology. The second part is "post-technology" and will deal with changes in the environment wrought by the technology, the status of the technology within the alliance, and the overall effect of the technology on the alliance.

ECONOMIC CHANGES

In contrast to the Europe of the postwar era, the economic vibrancy of Europe in the 1960s was remarkable. In part due to the efforts of the United States, a resurgent Europe had taken on a new economic life of its own, and the years of Western economic dominance by the United States were over. Formerly, the American dollar had been the foundation for the Western currency system. But by running a balance of payments deficit throughout the 1950s, the United States had seriously undermined foreign confidence in the dollar.[2] Unilateral efforts in strengthening it against the combined weight of European currencies had proved to be but temporary palliatives. Increasingly, the United States was forced to include Western Europe and Japan in the formulation of international economic policies. Without this support, such policies were doomed.

On European insistence, economic structures designed to widen the access to policy formulation were created starting in the early 1960s.[3] The inability of the United States to stem excessive speculation against the dollar was especially troubling, since the dollar and America's willingness to convert it to gold underpinned the Western monetary system. Consequently, the states of Europe formed the Group of Ten, which was to aid the International Monetary Fund, and in reality, the United States in combating excessive currency speculation by private investors. By 1969, after five years of negotiation, Special Drawing Rights, or "paper gold," were created as a new form of international liquidity. This new form of artificial international reserve units was to be managed not by the United States, but by the Group of Ten, for the Europeans had a veto power over the award of those rights.[4]

Pooling their economic strength, the major states of Western Europe had combined to form the European Economic Community (EEC) and soon negotiated favorable tariff reductions with the United States. When it was perceived that the United States was attempting to exert its influence on the EEC by sponsoring the entry of Great Britain, that membership (and with it the notion of continued American domination) was rejected throughout the 1960s.[5] Only after the EEC's independence from the United States had been clearly established was Great Britain allowed to join. If there were any traces of lingering doubt about the demise of the United States as the preeminent power of the Western economic system, the denouement came in August 1971, when America closed its "gold window."[6] By refusing to convert any further dollars to gold, the United States effectively scuttled the last vestiges of the postwar system of fixed exchange rates based on the dollar value of gold, and, hence, American hegemony in the Western international economic system.

Seeking to capitalize on their revitalized economic systems and on the decline in American economic hegemony, the major states of Western Europe began to forge economic ties with Eastern Europe and the Soviet Union. Tentatively at first, economic West met economic East.[7] This was a startling reversal of the Cold War–era policy of a virtual prohibition of trade with Communist bloc countries. This broadening of the Western European trade base was another step in the reduction of the dominant position of the United States. The strengthening of the economic ties between Eastern Europe and Asia was possible in part due to a further breakdown of the Old World order of the 1950s. The decline of the old economic order of the West had been accompanied by cracks in the ideological sphere of the East, allowing spans across the former political divide. Almost paradoxically, the increasing Soviet military power made those political interactions necessary and possible.

IDEOLOGICAL CRACKS

The economic revival of Europe and accompanying relative decline of the United States coincided with another change in the structure and distribution of power in the international political system. Perhaps more so than the term "West," "East" conjured up images of a cohesive group of states acting as one. Bonded together by seemingly unbreakable military, economic, and ideological ties, Communist states appeared to most Western scholars as an unshakable monolith. In the 1960s, it became clear that strains existed in that monolith. An increasingly bitter debate between the Soviet Union and People's Republic of China surfaced publicly in the 1960s.

On its surface, the debate centered around the desirability of "many roads to Communism" and the necessity of "peaceful co-existence" that had become a part of the Soviet doctrine since the mid–Khrushchev period.[8] For their part, the Chinese sought a more confrontational posture toward capitalism, rejecting the notion that conversion to the Communist system would come "from within." But these polemics were a subterfuge for the real basis of the conflict which lay in China's unwillingness to continue to subordinate itself to the Soviet Union. The Chinese Communist Party's real heresy was not its refusal to accept the doctrine of Karl Marx as interpreted by the Kremlin, but was the constant efforts by the party to establish an alternate source of attraction within the Communist movement.[9]

For the Soviets, the conflict had its roots in the historical animosity that state had displayed in its attempt to absorb a "backward" people on its Asia peripheries. To the proud descendants of the "Middle Kingdom," whose treasure had been plundered for centuries by Russians (among others), continued subservience was intolerable. By the end of the decade, the vituperation had escalated to armed attacks and reprisals by border patrols along the region of the Amur and Ussuri rivers in Manchuria. This animosity between the two giants of the Communist world was to provide for the United States an opportunity to lessen one of its more persistent foreign policy dilemmas—Vietnam.

By the late 1960s, the United States had averted its eyes from NATO and its problems of nuclear control, conventional force understrengths, and the credibility of the American strategic guarantee. Its major preoccupation was with events in Southeast Asia. The war in Vietnam had become a sump for America's resources, and a cleaver through the national consensus. For some, it was symbol of commitment by the United States to honor its obligations; for others, it was a symbol of imperial America compounding immorality with folly. Starting from a handful of military advisers in the early 1950s and peaking with the deployment in Vietnam of over 550,000 troops in mid 1968, the war absorbed a large measure of the United States defense budget, which necessarily detracted from that devoted to support of NATO. Troop and equipment levels were drawn down in the American units stationed in Europe in order to support the Vietnam effort. For those units remaining in Germany, the frequent reassignment of personnel caused by Vietnam requirements, coupled with an insufficient amount of equipment necessary for proper training, caused unit cohesion and readiness for combat to be degraded.[10] Since the United States supplied almost a third of the conventional forces in the Central Front of NATO, this decline in force capability was significant.

In addition to debilitating the capability of NATO, the American involvement in Vietnam had other, more indirect effects. Domestic reaction to the war in Vietnam was increasingly adverse by the late 1960s, and commitment of American troops anywhere (to include Europe) was in doubt. Seeking to reduce American commitments abroad as much as to silence domestic critics, the United States proclaimed a new doctrine of "self help," ostensibly for its Asian allies.[11] This policy of reduced material support and announced reluctance to commit American forces in Asia seemed to reflect a more pervasive attitude of "don't call us, we'll call you" toward all commitments. Given the recent controversy with NATO regarding the American-sponsored policy of "flexible response," the significance of this new doctrine was not lost on the European members of NATO. Further doubts of American constancy were fueled by efforts within the U.S. Senate to reduce American troop strength in Europe if other NATO members were not more forthcoming on burden sharing. In contrast to its former policy of attempting to "pay any price, bear any burden," in support of freedom, the United States was apparently not as anxious to commit either its tangible resources or its "honor" to some other state. For an alliance founded on the threat of the use of the ultimate of resources—the strategic guarantee of the United States against Soviet aggression in Europe—the new American policy was most troubling.

POLITICAL OPPORTUNITIES

China's break with the Soviet Union was to provide the United States with an opportunity to escape its Vietnam quagmire. Since the Chinese were anxious to counteract Soviet efforts at "hegemonism" and to gain economic and technological assistance available only from the industrialized democracies, they were willing, at least for the moment, to aid American efforts to escape from Vietnam. The overall American intent of this exercise in triangular diplomacy was to capitalize on the new international distribution of power and the American domestic situation by containing the Soviets with a Chinese counterpoise. A side effect, however, was that it posed additional problems for NATO.

In this effort at triangular diplomacy, the United States necessarily concentrated its diplomatic energies on its adversaries—the Soviet Union and the People's Republic of China. The result was a lack of attention to its allies—most significantly to NATO.[12] For example, London virtually was reduced to the status of a refueling point by senior American officials on trips to Moscow and Peking. The reduction of tensions between the superpowers (as evidenced by the vast increase in economic and cultural interactions) and the concentration by the American administration on its adversaries was to produce a debilitating effect on NATO. The case of Germany is instructive. Not content with an apparent stalemate in superpower efforts to solve its singular most urgent foreign policy problem and dubious of continued American leadership, Germany sought to follow the French lead and reassert itself internationally.

The Federal Republic of Germany had long pursued the goal of reunification. But that eventuality had depended upon the pleasure of the Soviets, for an armed Germany attempting reunification unilaterally by force would not be possible and would also raise the spectre of the Germany of old, which would be completely unacceptable to the other members of the alliance. Logic therefore dictated that reunification attempts should proceed peacefully. Accordingly, in early 1970, the Federal Republic of Germany initiated the *Ostpolitik* policy which was designed to reduce tensions with the Soviet Union and the German Democratic Republic.[13] By renouncing the use of force to achieve reunification, the Federal Republic agreed to accept the status quo, at least temporarily. In return for recognition of the German Democratic Republic, negotiations were to be undertaken on the Oder-Neisse borders and various arrangements concerning the status of Berlin and its occupying powers.

This policy was neither initiated nor controlled by the United States. It was the "inevitable" result of the restoration of the economic and political health of Germany. Although the United States attempted to weave *Ostpolitik* into a concerted allied policy vis-à-vis the Soviet Union, such actions were only partially successful. However, the conditions underlying the policy's initiation were clear; the Federal Republic of Germany was not under the political domination of the United States and did not feel compelled to consult on foreign policy matters of great substance beforehand. Also, a policy of accommodation with the Soviet Union was not the strict province of the United States. It was possible for other states to seek their security interests exclusive of American assistance. Such factors would naturally serve to erode the ties of NATO over time, for an alliance based on the fear of a Soviet attack could only wither with the antecedent condition removed.

SOVIET MILITARY STRENGTH

The Soviets had surprised Western intelligence analysts in 1949 by exploding an atomic bomb almost five years ahead of the analysts' predictions. Again, in 1953, they were ahead of Western analysts' schedule with the detonation of a hydrogen bomb. Starting in 1957, the Soviet Union dazzled an astonished world by launching a series of satellites into space. Initial American failures to duplicate those space feats soon prompted fears of a "missile gap" with the Soviet Union. Although the "gap" was the product of a rather severe "worst case" analysis of the Soviet production capabilities by these same intelligence experts, the efforts by the Soviet Union to achieve, at a minimum, a strategic military capability equal to that of the United States had begun.

For its part, the United States responded to the Soviet missile success of 1957 and the apparent "missile gap" by embarking upon its own ambitious strategic missile program, which quickly outdistanced the Soviets but leveled off in 1968. After the Cuban Missile Crisis, the Soviets redoubled their efforts in missile technology and slowly developed a variety of large missiles capable of carrying great payloads over intercontinental distances. By 1969, the trends were clear. The United States could not hope to maintain its strategic military superiority over the Soviet Union by merely increasing its own strength.[14] Because of the distribution of its budgetary resources, and the prevailing negative popular opinion toward military expenditures, it could no longer be the policy of the United States to rely on its "superiority" to deter the Soviet Union. Instead, officials determined it needed only "sufficient" strength to do so. This was no small change in strategic semantics, for it represented a clear shift in the balance of strategic forces. The implications of that word variation were not lost on NATO and cast further doubt on the credibility of the American strategic guarantee for Europe.

The growth of Soviet strategic power and its estrangement from China were also factors in the United States policy toward NATO. As it became clear that America would be unable to maintain its edge in strategic nuclear weaponry over the Soviet Union, the United States pursued a policy of relaxation of tensions, seeking to move "from an era of confrontation to an era of negotiation."[15] The culmination of this effort was the agreement to place limits on each country's strategic arsenal. This process, known as the Strategic Arms Limitation Treaty (SALT) talks, was the "centerpiece of détente" between the two superpowers. However beneficial it may have been to the two signatories, its effects on NATO were less favorable.

The Anti-Ballistic Missile (ABM) Treaty was particularly troubling to Europe. That treaty in effect guaranteed that both sides would suffer great civilian devastation in the event of strategic nuclear war. The assurance of mutual destruction was to ensure that strategic war would not be fought between the two superpowers. But what, the Europeans wondered, of war in Europe? If strategic war was now guaranteed to be too horrible, perhaps "limited war" must necessarily be confined to Europe—the strategic linkage was decoupled. Alternatively, perhaps rather than war, the two superpowers would conclude Europe's fate without a war—a superpower "condominium." Either scenario was unsatisfactory to Europeans, yet appeared to be codified by the ABM Treaty.

In an effort to shore up the cohesion of the alliance and to reassure its allies of the continued necessity for a strong alliance in an era of reduced tensions, the United States went on the diplomatic offensive. Declaring 1973 to be the "Year of Europe," the United States attempted to refurbish its ties with the alliance. Such efforts ended in disaster in October of that year, when the Organization for Petroleum Exporting Countries (OPEC) sharply raised its prices for oil and threatened not to supply those states supporting Israel in its war with Arab states. To ensure the continued flow of economic "blood," members of NATO quickly denied overflight and base-loading rights to American planes headed to Israel. The sight of American armored units shipping their tanks to Israel, thereby decreasing the already unfavorable NATO/Warsaw Pact tank balance, also prompted some NATO members to speculate as to the priority of American overseas commitments. Nor were they encouraged when scolded by Americans for their reluctance to provide support, or by vague threats of "agonizing reappraisals" of the American commitment to the alliance. For some, it was "the end of an era" of NATO and marked a watershed in relations among alliance members.[16] Rather than being a function of the 1973 Arab-Israeli War, this condition was merely the culmination of a long process begun when America first began to assert its dominance over the alliance. It was clear that forces in the environment had a deleterious effect on the alliance.

The international atmosphere, exemplified by SALT, MBFR (Mutual and Balanced Force Reductions in Europe), CSCE (Conference of Security and Cooperation in Europe), and expanding East/West trade is one of détente. When we add to this the rationale that the China threat limits the Soviet Union's flexibility to deploy its full potential against NATO, we must conclude that the foreseeable NATO environment is more conducive to decreased than increased spending.[17]

Partly because of these external forces, NATO had undergone significant change since its inception. These forces continued to buffet the alliance and some form of adaptation was required. Exacerbating the difficulties of the alliance, however, was the existence of other sources of strains within the alliance. Those internal strains will be the subject of the succeeding portion of this case study.

NOTES

1. Arnold Wolfers, Introduction to *Alliance Policy in the Cold War*, ed. Arnold Wolfers (Baltimore: Johns Hopkins University Press, 1959), p. 1.

2. A state's "balance of payments" is composed of two major parts: the balance of capital account, and the balance of trade. Although the United States ran a net surplus in its balance of trade (exported more than it imported) during the 1950s, that amount was more than offset by the deficit in the capital account. Grants and foreign military expenditures constituted the bulk of the dollar outflow. Although the term "balance of payments" had the connotation of equality, only rarely are the flows within or between the two accounts equal, or "in balance."

3. Joan Edelman Spero, *The Politics of International Economic Relations* (New York: St. Martin's Press, 1977), pp. 38–43.

4. Ibid., p. 43.

5. Seyom Brown, *New Forces in World Politics* (Washington, DC: The Brookings Institution, 1974), p. 30, and Henry A. Kissinger, *The Troubled Partnership* (Garden City, NY: Doubleday and Co., 1965; Anchor Books, 1966), p. 8.

6. Spero, *Politics of International Economic Relations*, pp. 49–50.

7. In 1960, exports from the West to Eastern bloc countries, including the Soviet Union, amounted to $1,502m. Thereafter, there existed an uninterrupted increase in the volume of trade, reaching $4,674m in 1971. Imports from the East rose similarly. See: U.S. Department of Commerce, Bureau of East-West Trade, *Selected U.S.S.R. and Eastern Europe Economic Data*, July 1973, p. 2.

8. This section on the Sino-Soviet split is from Brown, *New Forces*, p. 50.

9. It was as much China's increasing power—industrial and military, as well as ideological—as any other failing that led to the precipitous downfall of Soviet Premier Khrushchev in 1964. Recall that he was ousted from power in the party a few hours before the Chinese first detonated a nuclear device. The detonation had been widely speculated about in the weeks preceding it.

10. The decline in combat readiness and unit cohesion was not confined only to those American forces in Europe. The author was a member of a United States Army artillery unit in the United States in 1967. The normal policy was for a new lieutenant (that is, an officer in the initial entry point of his service) to remain in a unit for three to six months before he was reassigned to Vietnam. Enlisted soldiers fared little better. With that amount of personnel turbulence, it was very difficult to conduct any effective training or maintain it at a satisfactory level of performance. Additionally, there was almost a total absence of officers in the next two higher grades, compounding the training problems.

11. The Nixon doctrine, as this shift in policy was called, was enunciated in very brief form on 26 July 1969. See *New York Times*, 26 July 1969, p. 1. See also Melvin R. Laird, *The Nixon Doctrine* (Washington, DC: The American Enterprise Institute for Public Policy Research, 1972).

12. This critique of the Nixon-Kissinger era of foreign policy is from John Stoessinger, *Henry Kissinger: The Anguish of Power* (New York: W. W. Norton and Co., 1976).

13. The outlines of *Ostpolitik* are from Henry A. Kissinger, *White House Years* (Boston: Little, Brown and Co., 1979), p. 409.

14. Although Richard Nixon had campaigned for the American presidency by promising, among other things, a "clear-cut superiority" of American military strength over that of the Soviets, within a month in office it was clear that this goal was unattainable. See Marvin Kalb and Bernard Kalb, *Kissinger* (Boston: Little, Brown and Co., 1974), p. 107.

15. There were a number of factors prompting the United States to seek a slowing of the pace of the buildup of its strategic arms. Indeed, preliminary maneuverings for the actual negotiation of strategic arms limitations had begun before the United States had officially reassessed

the strategic trends between the superpowers. The Johnson administration had made progress toward initiation of arms limits talks, but had been thwarted by the Soviet invasion of Czechoslovakia in 1968. See John Newhouse, *Cold Dawn: The Story of SALT* (New York: Holt, Rinehart, and Winston, 1973).

16. See, for example, Irving Kristol, "NATO: End of an Era." *Wall Street Journal*, 16 November 1973, p. 14.

17. Ibid.

7

The Alliance in the 1970s: Continued Strains and New Technology

To report that in the early 1970s, there were strains within the NATO alliance would be to provoke the comment, "So what else is new?"[1] As previously recounted, the accommodation between the United States and the Soviet Union as symbolized in the SALT I agreement renewed European fears of a superpower understanding at the expense of Europe. At the same time, the relaxation of tensions between the two nuclear powers promised a reduced probability of Soviet attack. For Europe, there existed at the same instant a perception of a decreased likelihood of attack but a heightened fear of its consequences. This fear of war's consequences led Europe to be more concerned with efforts at deterring war in Europe than with efforts at fighting it, which was the increasing concern of the United States.

STRATEGY CONCERNS: CONTROL VERSUS CONFIDENCE

The United States had become fearful that reliance on its strategic nuclear weapons to deter a Soviet attack on Western Europe was not a credible policy. Its experience with Massive Retaliation in the 1950s had indicated that reliance on strategic weapons to deter all but the most serious of threats to America was ineffective. Such a strategy had not deterred Communist guerrilla action in Asia or Soviet provocations in Berlin, and had not prevented the North Koreans or the Chinese from the use of massive force in South Korea. In crisis after crisis, it was apparent that the United States would not risk the use of its strategic option—it was only a credible response in the most extreme circumstances, which were usually left unspecified.

Tactical nuclear weapons had also become somewhat of an "embarrassment" for the United States. Although it had purveyed tactical nuclear weapons as a substitute for its own and Europe's troops in the 1950s, by the 1960s the situation had changed markedly. By then, the Soviet Union also possessed tactical nuclear weapons to complement its strategic capability. The Soviet Union could therefore match NATO in its use of tactical nuclear weapons and the problem of control and management of the escalatory process became at the same time more difficult and more necessary. As discussed in the preceding case study, there existed many physical uncertainties associated with the use of tactical nuclear weapons. These physical uncertainties created political uncertainties because the ability to manage the level of violence was less certain. The "slope" toward a strategic exchange was deemed slippery indeed and was to be avoided, except under the most drastic of circumstances.

Therefore, in order to reduce reliance on the American strategic guarantee and to avoid the necessity for early use of tactical nuclear weapons with their attendant great collateral damage, the United States had pressed for a shift of emphasis from nuclear weapons to a strategy to bolster NATO's sagging conventional strength.[2] These forces had dwindled under the previous NATO strategy of reliance on the firepower of tactical nuclear weapons instead of conventional forces. It was feared that the very lack of conventional forces would leave NATO with no other option than to resort to tactical nuclear weapons. This initial use would then lead inexorably to the launching of strategic nuclear weapons from America—and a similar Soviet response—resulting in catastrophic effects on the whole world. More flexibility was needed at all levels—a flexibility to be provided by more conventional forces—so

that early resort to tactical nuclear weapons would not be necessary.[3]

Flexibility was also required in the application of the tactical
nuclear weapons themselves. Weapons of less explosive power
("smaller") and containing fewer radioactive contaminants
("cleaner") were required. And since the battle was to be fought
with clear regard to political limits in order to reduce the likelihood of escalation to strategic war, it would be necessary to retain
firm control over the employment of those nuclear weapons. That
is, the United States would continue to retain physical control
over the weapons even after they were approved for use. Since all
decisions regarding the employment of nuclear weapons required
unanimous consent of the NATO membership, the manner of this
use could be controlled. Therefore, the American finger was se-
curely on the tactical nuclear trigger. It was this notion of war-
fighting flexibility, which implied choice and exclusive American
control of nuclear weapons, that was so upsetting to the Europeans.[4]

To NATO Europe, the prospect of fighting a war in Europe
was most unappealing. It argued that because of overwhelming
Soviet conventional strength, NATO could hope only to delay
briefly a Soviet rush to the Rhine. NATO could never match the
Soviets with conventional forces, so instead should rely on the
American nuclear capability. Yet tactical nuclear weapons, no matter
how "clean" or "small," still possessed enormous destructive power
especially because of collateral destruction that would inevitably
result owing to Europe's high population density. These weapons
should be avoided as a war-fighting means. Instead, NATO's emphasis should be on the deterrence of war rather than options for
fighting it.

For Europe, "choice" was to be avoided. The linkage between
fighting in Europe and America's strategic forces was to be readily
apparent and indissoluble—almost automatic. Talk of "flexibility"
and "options" cast doubt among the Europeans as to the strength
of America's commitment and therefore, by extension, also cast
doubt in the minds of the Soviets. Thus, the very war which each
state sought to avoid would be encouraged by America's apparent
desire not to be forced into immediate support of Europe with

strategic weapons. Any benefit of flexibility in the war-fighting strategy of NATO also possessed the cost of corroding the deterrent effect of the alliance. In effect, then, Europe was demanding that the United States threaten to undergo what it was not prepared to do itself—nuclear destruction.

Europe was therefore faced with the task of influencing American policy and increasing its own security, both at the least cost. The United States' physical control over its tactical and strategic weapons enabled it to control their employment. Therefore, NATO Europe sought to reduce that flexibility and increase the deterrent capability of the alliance. By pleading budgetary problems and not developing its conventional forces, it hoped to force early resort to tactical, and then strategic, weaponry. This quick linkage to America's strategic arsenal was to guarantee the peace.[5]

On the other side of the Atlantic, the United States was increasingly doubtful of the efficacy of a pledge of its own nuclear destruction, yet equally desirous of maintaining that pledge in order to demonstrate its support for Europe and enhance alliance cohesion and efficacy. The United States was therefore in the awkward position of simultaneously encouraging its allies to devote more resources toward a policy that generated fears of American abandonment and which, if implemented, would likely destroy them, yet frequently having to demonstrate its constancy by repeating its adherence toward that policy which, if implemented, would likely destroy the United States. The constant repetition of this pledge gave NATO Europe the excuse it needed *not* to develop its conventional forces, and provided for Europe the method to ensure that pledge would be kept.

AMERICAN AND EUROPEAN BUDGETARY CONCERNS

Europe's contention that additional conventional forces would be deleterious to the deterrent effect of the alliance was motivated partly by budgetary problems. Although the economic revitalization of Europe had certainly occurred, there was serious domestic political opposition in Europe to increased defense spending during an era of an apparently declining threat. Undaunted, the United

States in the early 1970s embarked upon a campaign aimed at a more equitable distribution of alliance financial responsibilities. Called "burden sharing," it provided a handy smoke screen from which to dodge charges of a lack of American strategic commitment to NATO.

In many ways, burden sharing was linked to the U.S. involvement in Vietnam. As the war escalated in the mid 1960s, the United States had made incremental increases in men and materiel until it had committed over 535,000 ground troops to that area. Since the United States was also involved in expensive domestic social welfare, or "butter" programs, part of the "guns" resources had to come from elsewhere.[6] That "elsewhere" was Europe. Although the United States increased the amount of its defense budget to support the Vietnam effort, troops and equipment were drawn from Europe to aid in Vietnam. As the war effort began to wind down, the domestic reaction to continued high levels of defense spending was adverse and restoration of U.S. forces in Europe to their prewar levels of men and equipment was proving difficult.[7] In the early 1970s, serious efforts were made by the American Congress to reduce sharply the number of U.S. troops in Europe, but these efforts were barely defeated by virtue of strong administration arm-twisting.[8] Finally, in great measure to lessen domestic criticism of the military and of the military service caused by the Vietnam War (which endured despite American efforts to withdraw "with honor"), the United States abandoned mandatory military service and switched to a volunteer force, hoping to create a more disciplined, willing, motivated, professional force. Its effect in Europe was perceived as a further erosion of American will to defend Europe.[9]

Another source of tension within the alliance (and within the American Congress) was the fact that the United States was allocating a greater percentage of its gross national product (GNP) to its military establishment than most European states. America correctly argued that the economies of the member nations had long ago regained their health and a restructuring of the burden for support of NATO was deemed in order.

But the European nations were not without their share of difficulties.[10] France had withdrawn its forces from NATO in 1966, but remained a member in the non-military portion of NATO. It

100 New Weapons and NATO

had continued to devote approximately the same portion of its GNP to defense spending, and had developed a modest strategic force which could strike the Soviet Union. However, French forces were deleted from NATO defense planning and did not participate in NATO exercises. Although speculation persisted that the French would surely fight if NATO were attacked, their outright withdrawal and their lack of integrated training with other NATO forces reduced the cohesion and overall effectiveness of the alliance.

Difficulties on NATO's southern flank were also to plague the alliance. Greece and Turkey had clashed before over Cyprus and were to do so again in 1974. Vain attempts by the United States to solve those early crises only aided the friction between those states and increased their animosity toward the United States as well. In Italy, economic stagnation and the government's ineffective efforts to deal with it had caused that member to turn increasingly toward a branch of national Communism. Eurocommunism, as it was called, had made Italian domestic coalition building more difficult, although the Communist Party was never a member of the majority coalition. The fragility of that coalition was such that Italian governments usually were unable to gain sufficient support to establish stern measures to deal with the economic woes, with the resulting discontent leading to their downfall, thereby exacerbating the problem. The continuing economic difficulties affected Italy's ability to support its military establishment, and both the number of troops in active service and the percentage of the GNP devoted to defense continued to fall during the decade.[11]

To the North, Great Britain continued with grinding taxation—the apparent legacy of the Socialist effort—and double digit inflation. Militarily, the British Army of the Rhine was gradually reduced in strength as Great Britain sought to cut its military strength overall and use a portion of its forces to battle the terrorist war in Northern Ireland.

On the North German Plain, the Benelux countries were also suffering with attempts to finance social legislation and were less willing to maintain the status of their modest military establishments. To the north, Denmark reduced its force levels in seeking to hold the line on military spending, as did Norway.[12] Iceland, although contributing no military forces to NATO, had lent its territory as an important naval base for antisubmarine efforts by NATO. By the end of the 1970s, however, domestic discontent threatened to force the eventual closing of that base, thereby jeopardizing a major portion of the NATO antisubmarine warfare defense plan.[13]

By the 1970s, it was, as one author remarked, "common-place" to observe that the alliance was in disarray.[14] Domestic priorities had caused reductions in the military manpower level by NATO members and gradual reduction in the levels of defense spending, as shown in Appendix 1. This had come at a time when NATO had recently, if reluctantly, accepted the American-sponsored concept of "flexible response," which required an enhanced nuclear and conventional force capability by the alliance. Encumbered by its own economic woes and hampered by Vietnam, the United States complained about the inequitable distribution of the costs of maintaining the physical facilities of the alliance and its cost in stationing troops overseas. These complaints were countered by European members with comments about the lack of strategic commitment by the United States to defend NATO.

A TECHNOLOGICAL SOLUTION?

Since the debate over the status of conventional forces and of burden sharing outwardly concerned economics, and the United States was certain of its commitment to NATO, the problem ostensibly was one of greater military efficiency. In many respects, the problem of expensive military resources competing with domestic priorities was a replay of the situation facing the alliance in the early 1950s. Because of domestic budget priorities, NATO Europe was unable to field additional conventional forces at a time when domestic pressures in the United States were pushing for reduced levels of its forces in Europe. Then, as now, a possible partial solution to NATO's woes lay in the recent developments in military technology. A new family of weapons which were relatively inexpensive and very accurate held the possibility of providing an increase in conventional force effectiveness which would require fewer troops. Called precision-guided munitions (PGMs), this new family of weapons was seen by some military analysts to be the answer to NATO's problems.

Precise definitions of PGMs were difficult. James Digby's description of a PGM as "a munition whose probability of making a hit at full range . . . is greater than half" would apply to most weapons developed over the years.[15] An operational definition would appear to be either too general to be usable or too restricted to cover the field. Rather than attempting to define precision weaponry, a more useful course would be to cite their characteristics.

Precision-guided munitions are able to make in-flight corrections of their trajectory; they are thus very accurate, yet are relatively inexpensive. In-flight corrections to the weapon's trajectory may be made as a result of the "sensing" of required course changes by the weapon's onboard guidance equipment or by electrical commands from guidance equipment at the launch point. In either case, the weapon is able to receive these electrical stimuli and convert them into mechanical actions by onboard control equipment, thereby affecting the weapon's trajectory and resulting in greatly improved accuracy. The cost is considered low relative to that of a tank or short-range tactical missile, each costing more than $1 million. Individual PGMs may cost as little as $1,000, or as much as $100,000.[16] Although there is a significant amount of variance in this category, it is substantially less than the earlier attempts at precision guidance which were possible only on the larger, more complicated equipment costing millions of dollars.[17]

The characteristics of low cost and high accuracy were the major "selling" points of this new technology. There were other aspects, however, which were also attractive to the military analysts. The succeeding portion of this chapter will discuss those aspects and will be divided into two sections. Since PGMs were relatively novel, the first section will be concerned with a brief description of the types of precision weaponry available to the alliance. The second section will deal with the relationship of the precision-guided munitions to NATO. It will examine their compatibility with the current doctrine, their employment characteristics, and the political significance of their use.

PRECISION-GUIDED MUNITIONS—
A BRIEF LOOK

In looking at the development of precision weaponry, this study will be concerned with only a representative sample of the various weapons employing four major types of guidance techniques available for PGMs in the 1970s. A more thorough discussion of a larger number of PGMs may be found in the previously cited writings of James Digby. The tables in Appendixes 3, 4, and 5 briefly list performance characteristics of some weapons typical of the period and their origin of manufacture.

Operator-Guided PGMs

PGMs that required the launch operator to guide them to their target were the most common type of system and were the first type of PGMs to be developed. In the mid 1950s, France developed the *ENTAC* antitank missile. The operator fixed a simple sight on the target and relayed course corrections to the missile in flight via small wires trailing back to the launch point. This wire guidance technique remains in use today in many systems and has been supplemented by both radio command–guided systems that use radio signals and fiber optic cables instead of wires to transmit course corrections.

Seeker-Guided PGMs

Seeker-guided PGMs "home in" on the energy emissions of their target. Infrared, or heat seeking, PGMs were common. Usually used against aircraft, the in-flight missile detected the hot exhaust gases of its target and flew to that point. PGMs with radio frequency seeker guidance were usually employed against energy-emitting radar stations and radio antennae.

Laser-Guided PGMs

Weapon systems that utilized laser energy to guide them to their target were of more recent development, most coming since the mid 1970s. Laser-guided systems used a combination of the operator-guided and energy-seeker guidance systems described above. The target was "illuminated" by a laser beam of energy and the in-flight PGM homed in on the illuminated object.

TV-Guided Systems

Another recent development in PGM guidance was the development of television-guided systems. Essentially using a television screen with cross hairs superimposed on the screen, the operator scanned the target area with a television camera, placed the cross hairs on the desired target, and fired the projectile. The PGM, employing its own camera, flew to the point indicated by the cross hairs.

Appendixes 3, 4, and 5 provide additional information on other selected PGM systems in use or anticipated to be fielded in the 1970s. It will be noted from the tables that the distribution of precision-guided munition users within the alliance was limited to only a few members—notably the United States, Great Britain, France, and Germany. This fact and its implications for the alliance will be discussed later.

In discussing the various types of guidance techniques available for employment in precision-guided munitions, one might well wonder how anything or anybody could withstand the deadly accuracy of PGMs. It would appear that the PGMs might well cause a change in the conduct of warfare. However, in actual combat, precision-guided munitions have been employed only in limited numbers and under close to ideal conditions of terrain and weather. Whatever the early claims of their manufacturers, it is now clear that the effectiveness of precision weaponry can be degraded by an opponent's use of them, by revisions in weapons design and military tactics to offset the weapon's efficiency, and by differing conditions of terrain and weather. Early assessment of the pros and cons of the effectiveness of precision weaponry and consequent implications for warfare was vigorous, yet inconclusive.[18] This much was clear: PGMs were more effective than their "dumb" cousins, inexpensive, and available. Therefore, let us turn to an examination of the relationship of PGMs to NATO. How did they relate to the current military strategy? What were the political implications of their use? Were specialized decision-making structures required to approve their employment?

PRECISION-GUIDED MUNITIONS AND NATO

Precision-guided munitions seemed to possess all the benefits that the previous new weapon technologies did not. Unlike tactical nuclear weapons, precision weaponry did not cause vast amounts of collateral damage when used. They did not possess radioactive components and therefore did not pose a health hazard to noncombatants many miles from the battle area. Although they were a new form of weaponry, there did not immediately develop a tradition of non-use, as has occurred with tactical nuclear weapons and biological agents. In many respects, precision-guided munitions seemed to be the ideal new technology for NATO.

During a period of increasing inability by member states to maintain their military force levels in NATO because of other budgetary priorities, precision weaponry with its low cost and high accuracy had a high payoff in military efficiency. Although the size of the "bang" was the same, more hits could be achieved for fewer "bucks" than with the non-precision ("dumb") munitions. Since this new technology was conventional (non-nuclear) in nature, it was in consonance with the thrust of the recently adopted NATO strategy of "flexible response." The alliance's conventional force capability would be enhanced in order to deter the initial attack, and, that failing, PGM use would preclude the great amounts of damage that would be wrought by a nuclear war, even "limited" to the degree foreseen by some. Additionally, an increased conventional capability would allow NATO to meet Soviet/Warsaw Pact aggression without the strain imposed by the decision to resort to tactical nuclear weapons. That is, it would provide an alternative war-fighting option to tactical nuclear weapons and thereby reduce the corrosive effects on the alliance caused by the American control of tactical nuclear weapons.

Precision-guided munitions fit other aspects of the "flexible response" strategy of the alliance very well. Most of the precision weaponry developed over the decade was designed to be employed with conventional explosives.[19] This was mainly due to the high accuracy of the weapon, which allowed it to destroy its target without an excess of explosive power. Previously, additional explosive power was required in order to achieve the desired degree of damage to the target by hitting or detonating close by. The closer the explosion to the target, the less explosive force was required to destroy it. Therefore, not only did PGMs not use nuclear warheads, they employed less powerful conventional warheads than before. Additionally, their high accuracy meant that fewer non-military targets would be hit. All these factors augured for a reduced amount of damage, especially to non-military targets, again complementing the "flexible response" strategy of NATO.

Another benefit of the non-nuclear explosives employed with precision munitions was that high-level authority for employment was not needed. The Nuclear Planning Group and the Nuclear Defense Affairs Committee, which were created in order to facilitate the planning for, and hence the release of, nuclear weapons, were not concerned with precision weapons. As conventional weapons, precision munitions were authorized for use routinely as the local military commander saw fit. Therefore, the issue of American control of these weapons was not a problem for NATO members in the manner that it was for tactical nuclear weapons. This was a further "plus" for the compatibility of precision munitions with the current military strategy and governing structure.

There were other benefits as well. Since the Soviet Union did not possess this new technology to the degree that some of the members of NATO did, military analysts (mostly American) saw its deployment as a means of capitalizing on this technological advantage and offsetting the Soviet/Warsaw Pact preponderance of firepower. This increase was thought to provide at least a partial redress of the balance of conventional forces and was seen as a means of shoring up the deterrence aspect of NATO's strategy. Additionally, since the technology was fairly well known among manufacturers, the issue of American control of these weapons was obviated. Subject to national export licenses and their actual cost, the way was clear for diffusion of these weapons throughout the alliance.

Because they employed conventional explosives, precision-guided munitions did not detonate very much differently than their less-precise predecessors. There was no distinctive flash, radiation emission, or towering mushroom-like cloud as was normally associated with the detonation of a nuclear weapon. The size, color, and shape of the burst were the same as the conventional explosives then in use. In every physical way, then, precision-guided munitions were identical to their conventional predecessors, and were fully compatible with NATO plans and decision-making structures then in being. Therefore, they seemed ideally suited to avoid the pitfalls associated with the previous new technology of tactical nuclear weapons. In short, precision-guided munitions had "the right stuff" for at least a partial solution to NATO's military ills.

But what seems "right" and what actually occurs are sometimes two different matters. To what degree was this new technology distributed within the alliance? What was the overall effect of these weapons on the functioning and cohesion of NATO? These are some of the matters we will examine in the next chapter.

NOTES

1. Frank R. Barnett, Forward to "Nuclear Weapons and the Atlantic Alliance," by Wynfred Joshua (New York: National Strategy Information Center, Inc., 1973), p. v.

2. The phase "shift in emphasis" from the problem of strategic deterrence is not meant to imply that conventional force capabilities had been ignored previously or that strategic deterrence would subsequently be ignored, for neither was the case. Rather, the balance in strategic nuclear systems drew attention to the inequalities at the other levels.

3. This was the strategy of "flexible response" which was proposed by the Kennedy administration in 1961. The version approved in 1967 placed less emphasis on conventional forces and more emphasis on the nuclear aspects of the strategy.

4. Klauss Knorr, "The Atlantic Alliance: A Reappraisal," *Headline Series*, No. 221 (New York: Foreign Policy Association, 1974), p. 26.

5. The respected International Institute for Strategic Studies characterized NATO Europe's actions as follows: "Inevitably, therefore, they have been disinclined to find the material resources for full-scale conventional defense, simply because to do so would imply the possibility of limiting conflict to conventional war in Europe itself, without the neces-

sary transition to the strategic, intercontinental level. In a very real way, Western European members of NATO have depended upon a margin of conventional inadequacy to deter attack." For Europe, peace is not achieved through strength, but through weakness. *Strategic Survey 1972* (London: International Institute for Strategic Studies, 1973), p. 19. See also Irving Kristol, "NATO: The End of An Era," *Wall Street Journal*, 16 November 1973, p. 14.

6. To be sure, the annual Department of Defense budget increased during the years of the American involvement in Vietnam, going from 8.2 percent of the GNP in 1964 to 9.3 percent of the GNP in 1968 (the year of greatest military involvement in Vietnam). However, as has been discussed, a portion of the U.S. commitment to Vietnam came from its forces stationed in NATO.

7. This is particularly true since the U.S. defense budgets were approximately 8 percent to 9 percent of the GNP during the earlier portion of the 1960s and postwar budgets were reduced from those levels.

8. Henry A. Kissinger, *White House Years* (Boston: Little, Brown, and Co., 1979), P. 938.

9. European perceptions are reported by Trevor Cliffe, "Military Technology and the European Balance," *Adelphi Papers*, No. 89 (London: International Institute for Strategic Studies, 1972); Andrew J. Pierre, "Can Europe's Security Be 'Decoupled' from America's?," *Foreign Affairs* 51 (July 1973): 761; and Francoise Duchene, "A New European Defense Community," *Foreign Affairs* 50 (October 1971): 69.

10. Data for the status of NATO Europe during the early 1970s are from R. C. Richardson, "Can NATO Fashion a New Strategy?," *Orbis* 17 (Summer 1973): 419; Robert W. Komer, "Treating NATO's Self-Inflicted Wound," *Foreign Policy* 13 (Winter 1973/1974): passim; Zbigniew Brzezinski, "The Deceptive Structure of Peace," *Foreign Policy* 14 (Spring 1974): 53; Kissinger, *White House Years*, p. 401; William P. Lineberry, *The U.S. in World Affairs 1970* (New York: Simon and Schuster, 1972), p. 223; Richard P. Stebbins, *The U.S. in World Affairs 1967* (New York: Simon and Schuster, 1968), p. 198: and Paul-Henri Spaak, *The Crisis of the Atlantic Alliance* (Columbus: Ohio State University Press, 1967).

11. See Appendix 1.

12. Erik B. Johansen, "On NATO's Northern Flank," *Military Review* 51 (August 1971): 63.

13. Ake Sparring, "Iceland, Europe and NATO," *The World Today* 28 (September 1972): 393.

14. Barnett in Joshua, "Nuclear Weapons and the Atlantic Alliance," p. v.

15. James Digby, "Precision-Guided Weapons," *Adelphi Papers*, No. 118 (London: International Institute for Strategic Studies, 1975), p. 7.

16. The cost of weaponry is deceptive. A particular piece of hardware may have an "off-the-shelf" cost of a few thousand dollars if purchased from the established maufacturer. For a new company to start from "scratch" and attempt to build that piece of hardware, the cost would be much higher. Additionally, weapons purchases have hidden costs. For example, it has been said that the TOW antitank missile has a low cost—$3000 per missile. However, the cost of the missile is not the entire cost. The cost of the computer ($20,000 in 1975) and the launcher with its complex optical equipment must also be considered. Also, spare parts, training equipment, training of maintenance personnel, and much more must be considered in the "cost" of a weapon. Still, PGMs are relatively inexpensive.

17. For example, the U.S. Pershing missile was developed in the early 1960s at a cost of approximately $6 million per missile. It was inertially guided—that is, onboard guidance computers could detect the missile's deviation from a preplanned flight path and cause the missile to alter its trajectory to that of the correct, predicted flight path. Though possessing the first PGM characteristic of in-flight correction capability, it failed the second criterion of cost.

18. Some participants in the debate were: J. D. Lunt, "A Commentary on the Fourth Arab-Israeli War," *The Army Quarterly and Defense Journal* 104 (January 1974): 168–71; Edgar O'Ballance, "The Fifth Arab-Israeli War—October 1973," *The Army Quarterly and Defense Journal* 104 (April 1974): 308; Martin van Creveld, *Military Lessons of the Yom Kippur War: Historical Perspectives*, The Washington Press, No. 24 (Beverly Hills/London: Sage Publications, 1975); Digby, "Precision-Guided Weapons;" Richard A. Burt, "The Debate on the New Weapons Technology," *Adelphi Papers*, No. 126 (London: International Institute for Strategic Studies, 1976); The Insight Team of the London *Sunday Times, The Yom Kippur War* (Garden City, NY: Doubleday and Co., Inc., 1974); A. Merglen, "Military Lessons of the October War," in "The Middle East and the International System," *Adelphi Papers*, No. 114 (London: International Institute for Strategic Studies, Spring 1975), pp. 26–30; James Digby and Edison M. Cesar, Jr., "Utilization of Modern Weapons Suitable for Europe (U)" (Santa Monica, CA: Rand, 1978) SECRET; and Steven Canby, "The Alliance and Europe: Part IV, Military Doctrine and Technology," *Adelphi Papers*, No. 109 (London: International Institute for Strategic Studies, Winter 1974–1975).

19. A few of the larger, nuclear-capable weapon systems have employed components of precision guidance. The U.S. Army's nuclear-tipped

Pershing missile, while too expensive to be classed as a precision-guided munition for our purposes, has been developed with a radar correlation guidance system which matches radar-detected images with previously stored images. It then flies to the target superimposed on its radar-corrected "memory."

8

Precision-Guided Munitions and NATO in the 1970s: Mixed Results

"Too large to be a trip wire, too small to resist an all-out Soviet onslaught, the allied military establishment was an accidental array of forces in search of a mission."[1] While obviously overstated, Henry Kissinger's characterization of NATO's dilemma bears much truth. Because of their reliance on the United States for the ultimate in military support, European alliance members were increasingly reluctant to undertake an expensive conventional force buildup having no visible output in the face of other, much more tangible problems. The tough realities of scarce resources had forced difficult choices between the requirements of the alliance which produced "security" in a decreasingly tense world, and the requirements of social welfare programs, which produced tangible benefits to an increasingly expectant polity.

The promise of a new weapon technology to provide some relief to those problems was intriguing. Precision-guided munitions (PGMs) were offered to provide increased combat effectiveness at a bearable cost. It was hoped that this enhanced military capability might be the means whereby the prescribed force level requirements of the alliance could be met in a manner dictated by alliance strategy and acceptable to all. By solving a major problem, in an agreeable manner, greater alliance efficacy and cohesion would result. By reducing one of the "costs" of membership in the alliance, perhaps it could weather this latest economic storm. But the manner in which this new weapon technology was received (or, ultimately not received) was partly a function of forces external to the alliance, forces which had buffeted it in the early part of the decade and continued unabated. The détente process continued to encourage varying degrees of Western rapprochement with Moscow and adverse global economic trends fostered criticism of American leadership, while in response the United States speculated aloud about the constancy of its allies. It was in many ways alliance business as usual.

EXTRA-ALLIANCE CONCERNS

The process of relaxation of tensions between the Soviet Union and the United States which had begun in earnest in the early 1970s continued through most of the decade, albeit with a number of fits and starts. Upon conclusion of a treaty limiting the strategic arms of the two nuclear giants, negotiations continued, and in 1974 sufficient progress had been made to enable American officials to proclaim that a "cap" had been placed on the strategic arms race.[2] By the end of the decade, another agreement provided for a small reduction in some types of strategic nuclear weaponry, and overall limits on the quantity of other types.[3]

For its part, the United States was anxious to conclude a treaty limiting the growth of Soviet strategic forces. The Soviet Union had increased its strategic nuclear forces to such a level that by the end of the decade American officials were speaking of a "window of vulnerability" for the United States in the mid 1980s.[4] If Europeans were dubious of the American strategic guarantee in a period of "sufficiency" or "parity," it is not difficult to imagine their thought during a period of "vulnerability."[5]

The Soviet Union continued to develop its forces and doctrine to support offensive operations. Writings on Soviet military strategy and training exercises emphasized the defense of Warsaw Pact territory through theaterwide offensive actions designed to destroy NATO forces and seize NATO territory. These objectives were applicable to both nuclear and conventional conflict. Although nuclear war was not the inevitable result of conflict in Europe, it was deemed likely and Soviet forces were trained on employment of types of "weapons of mass destruction" to keep pressure on NATO forces. Indeed, the Soviet military machine appeared ready to fight, survive, and win on a conventional or nuclear battlefield.[6] The trends in Soviet and Warsaw Pact equipment levels and training exercises supporting this view continued through the decade. The increasing Soviet military power obviously made NATO's task of countering that buildup more formidable. It was also less attractive during a period when domestic programs were causing a reordering of budgetary priorities away from NATO defense spending.

In order to defuse the increasingly vocal expressions of discontent by NATO Europe about being excluded from matters deemed essential to its survival, and to gain its support for SALT II, the United States belatedly agreed to European participation in SALT III. That forum essentially was to consider those matters formerly under consideration in the stalled Mutual and Balanced Force Reduction talks.[7] However, even though the United States made this attempt to respond to the increasing reluctance of its NATO allies to allow America to continue to arrange the terms of their security, the die of unilateral action by individual members had been cast in other areas much earlier.

The United States policy of détente with the Soviets had encouraged the Europeans to continue apace with their individual versions of rapprochement. With the decline in its fears of a rearmed and reunited Germany, France undertook a leading role in the European interactions with the Soviet Union and its allies, especially in Eastern Europe. It did this in a fashion calculated to demonstrate to all that it had its own particular interests and was no longer content with American leadership.[8] The Federal Republic of Germany, still wary about taking on an increased international role lest old fears of German nationalism be revived, had nonetheless made diplomatic forays to Moscow to continue the decade-long policy of *Ostpolitik*. Such initiatives by Germany were encouraged by France as a part of its continuing policy of increasing the independence of Europe from Washington. In 1980, the French president could call for a "renaissance of European influence" and a "reappearance of an independent and self-assured Europe in world affairs."[9] This call for independence came less than six months after Europe had only weakly responded to vigorous American efforts to generate support for sanctions against the Soviet Union after its incursion into Afghanistan. It preceded a similarly weak response to American concerns over Poland.[10]

The economic reverberations caused by the 1973 oil price increase and threats of production slowdown were also a source of alliance disunity. The United States support of Israel brought it into confrontation with the Arab oil-producing states of the Persian Gulf region. Anxious to avoid an interruption of the supply of energy upon which it depended and having real differences with the American support of Israel, NATO Europe was reluctant to provide political or logistical support to U.S. efforts to aid Israel. Also, NATO members could rightfully claim that events in the Middle East were outside the legally defined jurisdiction of NATO and therefore did not require their concerted action. Thus, they were not inclined to support U.S. efforts at projecting a united front of consumers to counterbalance OPEC and sought instead to arrange unilaterally for their individual supplies of oil. Neither vague rumblings of "agonizing reappraisals" of American relations with its NATO allies nor the American president's warning to NATO Europe that it could not have "cooperation on the security front and then proceed to have confrontation and even hostilities on the economic and political front" did much to soothe the matter.[11]

Economic policies of the United States designed to smooth troubled waters with its allies were equally futile. In the late 1970s, conferences among the political leaders of the major economic states of NATO and Japan produced calls by the United States for those states to reduce their exports to the United States and thus help alleviate U.S. unemployment problems.[12] At the same time, the United States was not inclined to take action to support the dollar against other currencies, notably the Japanese yen and the German mark. America preferred to continue to import large quantities of oil, paying for it with increasingly less valuable dollars, thereby driving up the price of oil. Naturally, the pleas of the United States for reduction of foreign imports fell on deaf ears and its major economic partners continued to pursue their own policies, while the United States could only protest.

Thus, the yearly meetings of the heads of the major economic states of the West to compose policies to combat their common economic problems were little more than exercises in public relations. Promises would be made to meet particular goals, glowing communiqués proclaiming that tough new proposals would be released, and each state would pursue its own interests as soon as the meeting was over. The cost of such a charade was a deterioration of the American economic leadership role and an overall blow to the relations of industrial states.[13]

The inability of the major economic partners to agree on and pursue a unified economic and energy policy was reflective of the trends that had been born with the resurgence of the economic health of the states of Europe, and which had continued apace in the 1970s. It stood in sharp contrast to the days of the "dollar gap" and the Marshall Plan, when the United States was able to dominate the Western economic system.

Clearly, the ancien régime was no more. The economic capability of Europe had been restored from the post–World War II era and America was now having serious difficulties with budget deficits, unemployment, high interest rates, low productivity, and weak national growth. The resulting change in the distribution of economic power within the Western democracies had all but eliminated the leadership role of the United States in the Western economic system. The resurgent economic health and the increasingly suspect strategic military security provided by the United States had fostered the political recovery of Europe. Increasingly internationalist, the major states of Europe were much less willing to accept American leadership, or at least American counsel.

While it was fashionable to blame the decline of American leadership and the disarray of the Western democracies on a lack of leadership in Washington, the forces which brought about these changes in the distribution of power within the West existed independently of any particular occupant of the White House. The increasing degree of dependence of the Western states on external sources of vital resources, especially oil, was brought about by their very success in developing technology-dependent economies. This dependence had a leveling effect on all, which was not to be confused with a unifying effect. The reduction in the relative economic power of the United States and concomitant rise by the major states of Western Europe did not cause those states to coalesce, especially as regards a common economic policy vis-à-vis OPEC. Rather, each state sought its individual arrangements with its supplier.[14]

However, the increasing economic capacity of the European states did not make them any more willing to maintain, much less increase, their force levels committed to NATO. Europe remained unwilling to devote resources to develop conventional forces to be used against a foe it did not believe would attack.[15] The result was the continued decline of NATO's military power relative to the Soviet Union. All this was in spite of American pleas to the contrary and the promise of PGMs. Given these conditions in the alliance's environment, let us examine the status of precision-guided munitions within the alliance at the end of decade and then assess their effect thereon.

PRECISION-GUIDED MUNITIONS WITHIN NATO

The problems facing the military planners of the alliance were real. An era of declining defense spending and a general relaxation of tensions between East and West (if those terms even remained meaningful in a multipolar world) occurred during a period of buildup of Soviet/Warsaw Pact conventional forces. As a possible solution to the problem, precision-guided munitions offered some hope. This new weapon technology was widely available for distribution and seemed an attractive solution to alliance problems.

Unlike nuclear weapons, precision-guided munitions were not the exclusive province of the United States. The technology for their development existed in the major industrialized states of Europe and, to some degree, was employed in the development of precision-guided munitions there. But, by far, the United States dominated the field in the technology required in the development of precision weaponry.[16] The dominance existed in the state of the art and in the breadth of its application. The American effort in the exploration of space depended upon the advances in the development of microelectronics and microprocessors.[17] It was these components that were the basis for the guidance systems for most of the types of precision-guided munitions.

With such a rich base from which to draw, the incorporation of this space-related technology into the development of weapons of great accuracy was quite rapid and the number of American firms providing such weaponry proliferated. This was in stark contrast to the development of tactical nuclear weapons in the 1950s. That technology was a state secret and did not proliferate. The technology for precision-guided munitions was much more diffuse. Not only did a number of American firms adapt this technology to weaponry, but firms in other states did as well. However, their adoption of this technology was usually more limited than that by the American firms.

Many firms in NATO Europe incorporated the technology in their development of weaponry, but only on a limited variety of weapons.[18] Additionally, only to a limited extent did the United States enter into coproduction efforts or authorize production rights for some of the weaponry developed by American firms. In general, the technology for the development of precision-guided munitions was dispersed within NATO, but largely confined to the more advanced industrialized states such as Great Britain, France, Italy, and the United States.[19] Within that group, the United States had a clearer edge in the number of firms capable of producing such weaponry and in the variety of weapons produced. Although the sale of weaponry to foreign states required governmental approval, the United States government did not restrict the proliferation of precision-guided munitions to its NATO allies. Given this availability of the technology for precision weaponry, speculation on the manner and extent of its distribution commenced.[20]

Since PGMs had been used only occasionally in combat, some controversy existed as to the actual significance of the results. Based on different interpretations of the results, different consequences of the employment of these weapons resulted. Some authors foresaw increased manpower requirements; others, less.[21] Some foresaw increased logistical requirements; others, less.[22] Most foresaw some change to the strategy for the employment of conventional forces using these weapons, but the strategies varied.[23]

These visions of the PGM world of the future shared the same fault. They all assumed that precision-guided munitions would be fully incorporated into NATO's force structures. But such was not the case in the decade that precision weaponry was advertised and available. The basis for this judgment was rooted in the status of the alliance's environment and the orientation of the various members of the alliance toward the overall purpose of NATO.

This divergence of views was deeply rooted in a number of factors and caused the distribution of precision-guided munitions within the alliance to be neither uniform nor extensive. Rather than the vast reorganization of the various force structures, the great savings in manpower and equipment, the decreased logistical "tail" envisioned by proponents of precision-guided munitions, nothing of this sort materialized.

As the leading proponent and source of precision-guided weaponry, and as a state that preferred "hi-tech" or quality to quantity in military equipment, the United States deployed precision-guided munitions to the greatest degree among the members of the alliance. However, they were sought only as modernized replacements to existing weaponry. There was no wholesale precision-guided munition "binge" envisioned earlier by some of the more imaginative proponents. Unlike the World War II creation of antitank battalions armed with a high velocity gun, there was no creation of separate units organized around the employment of precision weaponry. Nor did any major reorganization of existing military structures occur in order to accommodate precision weaponry. Where precision weaponry was phased into American force structures, it usually replaced in kind less sophisticated models of equipment.[24] In some cases, however, the new weaponry augmented existing systems, serving to enhance their capability but not replace them.[25] In sum, there was less than the spectacular proliferation of precision weaponry envisioned by some, and certainly not the "Great 'Robot' Arms Race" postulated by others.[26]

If it can be said that the United States had not wholly embraced precision weaponry, the same observation may be made about its NATO allies. United States forces deployed precision weaponry to a much greater degree than did the remainder of the alliance. To illustrate, by the late 1970s, the United States possessed slightly less than three-fourths of all the types of antitank guided missile launchers (the new precision-guided antitank munitions) possessed by all the members of NATO.[27] France possessed almost 15 percent of the total and most of these were of the mid-1960s vintage. Given the improvements in armor protection employed in the

Warsaw Pact tanks developed since then, a major portion of France's present stock of antitank missiles was largely ineffective.

The remaining 10 percent of the NATO arsenal of antitank guided missiles was scattered among five other countries. That is, by the late 1970s, eight of the fifteen states of NATO did not possess any of the most common variety of precision weaponry. Given that the tank ratio between NATO and the Warsaw Pact was (and remains) one of NATO's most serious military problems, one would expect that the relatively inexpensive, very effective antitank guided missile would be sought by all members of the alliance in order to offset the Pact tank advantage. Clearly, that was not the case. Nor did it appear that the situation would soon change. Projections of the distribution of antitank guided missiles within the alliance to 1986 did not show much of a change from the mid 1970s. The United States would continue to incorporate antitank guided missiles into its arsenal, but at a decreasing rate, and NATO Europe would continue to lag far behind, with the bulk of the precision weaponry concentrated in a few major states.

To a lesser degree, the same situation of non-acceptance occurred with another form of precision weaponry.[28] Military analysts hoped that short-range, surface-to-air missiles would aid in offsetting the Warsaw Pact's advantage in tactical aircraft. The development of an active homing capability made highly accurate, man-portable missiles an inexpensive means of providing protection to ground troops from hostile aircraft. As with other forms of precision weaponry, the United States took the lead in employing this new technology and integrated small teams armed with these missiles into its conventional force structures. The teams were composed of three personnel and were assigned one to a company (160-man tactical unit). In this case, this new technology weapon increased personnel and logistical requirements of the force structure, but only to a small degree. Some other changes to the organizational structure occurred, but these too, were slight.

Within NATO, by the late 1970s, the United States possessed the greatest percentage of short-range, surface-to-air missiles. Over 50 percent belonged to the American forces stationed in Europe and 30 percent belonged to the Federal Republic of Germany. The remaining 20 percent were scattered within the British, French, and Canadian forces. Despite the edge in tactical aircraft possessed by the Soviet/Warsaw Pact forces, the eleven remaining nations of NATO did not possess any form of this low cost, available surface-to-air missile.

While the examples described above are but two in number, they are significant for two reasons. First, they involved situations where NATO had a distinct inferiority in a critical area. Second, the means of rectifying those deficiencies existed for some time. Therefore, one must conclude that if NATO members were disposed to take advantage of the benefits of the new weapon technology, they would have done it, at a minimum, in the two areas of antitank guided missiles and surface-to-air missiles. But clearly such was not the case in these specific instances and neither was it the case with precision-guided munitions in general. In all categories of weapons, precision-guided munitions were not acquired in the large amounts postulated by their scholarly and military proponents, nor were they distributed evenly within NATO.

Of the totals of precision weapons located in NATO Europe, the United States had by far the largest percentage of those weapons. The remaining portions of those totals were divided among a few other states of the alliance, with many states possessing none (or next to none) of the new type of weapons. Additionally, five-year projections continued to show little change in this situation. With this status of the distribution of precision weaponry with the alliance now established, let us turn to an overall assessment of their effect on NATO.

PRECISION-GUIDED MUNITIONS: AN ASSESSMENT

Alliance members had grown increasingly reluctant to provide the same level of military support to NATO during a period of sustained growth of Soviet conventional and strategic forces. For military planners thus faced with the problem of doing more with less, PGMs seemed to provide at least some of the answers to NATO's military ills. Military journals blossomed with predictions of a revolution in warfare and the breath of life for an increasingly divided NATO.

But such was not the case. Fully ten years after their widespread appearance, precision-guided munitions were not fully incorporated within NATO and the problems which divided alliance members before also remained unremedied. For an alliance facing an opponent engaged in a determined buildup of conventional forces, NATO did not choose to turn to precision munitions as a solution. Despite earlier, optimistic predictions for PGMs, their actual effects within NATO were much different. An assessment of these effects may be divided into two categories: military and political.

Military Effects

The maldistribution of precision-guided munitions within the alliance caused no real difficulties militarily. There was always a disparity in the military capability of the various national units and, indeed, within national units. Armored divisions, for example, inherently possessed more military capability (firepower and mobility in particular) than did infantry divisions. The existence of PGM-equipped forces alongside non-PGM forces posed no unusual difficulties for military planners, for the size of the assigned area of operations for a particular unit could be varied, depending upon the military capability of the unit. Additionally, because the explosive effects of precision munitions were fairly limited, especially in comparison to those of nuclear weapons, no special coordination between and among units was required in order to employ PGMs. The impact on logistical and personnel systems by precision munitions was somewhat mixed. With some munitions, the burdens on those systems were eased; in others, they increased. However, there was no increase in logistical supplies or personnel in the various force structures because of anticipated higher usage and casualty rates in the event of war.[29] This would have been true even if precision weaponry had been adopted on a more widespread basis. This is because no member of NATO has been prepared in peacetime to increase its logistical or personnel strengths to accommodate a predicted higher wartime usage rate. The case of tactical nuclear weapons is instructive. When fielded in Europe in the 1950s, most analysts agreed that war fought with these weapons would be far more destructive than any previous conflict. Despite these predictions, NATO members did not increase their logistics and personnel bases. Indeed, the opposite occurred. If the specter of the destruction of tactical nuclear warfare was not sufficient to invigorate logistics and personnel bases, precision-guided munitions were not either. There was not the same aura surrounding their use and therefore, they did not cause significant change to those support bases.

Because of their accuracy and non-nuclear nature, PGMs complemented NATO's strategy of "flexible response." That strategy called for the enhancement of the conventional war-fighting capacity of the alliance, and precision-guided munitions certainly were capable of that. Strategy debates which did arise concerning the employment of precision weaponry were ones essentially concerned with the optimum military tactics involved. There was nothing approaching a fundamental change in NATO strategy—merely a fine tuning of "flexible response." Nor were any structural changes to the alliance considered by its members. Because PGMs employed conventional explosives currently in use, no changes to existing planning agencies or decision-making bodies were made. In general, PGMs "fit" nicely into existing planning, command, and control arrangements.

In summary, then, precision-guided munitions had little effect on the military aspects of the alliance. In part, this was due to the nature of the new technology and in part to the extent of its distribution within the alliance. Because of their non-nuclear status, precision weapons were fully compatible with the military doctrine of "flexible response," and existing decision-making structures of the alliance were adequate to incorporate the inclusion of the new technology. This would have been true even if the density of precision weaponry within the alliance increased.

Political Effects

A significant shift toward the use of precision weaponry by the European members of the alliance did not occur for a number of reasons. The nature of the Soviet threat, the domestic political situations in the nations of the alliance, and the divergence of interests between alliance members as it relates to the military strategy and, ultimately, the purpose of NATO, suggest this conclusion.

The declining sense of threat felt by NATO Europe began after the Cuban Missile Crisis in 1962. From that event there flowed a number of mutually beneficial political agreements between the United States and the Soviet Union that seemed quite implausible a decade earlier. This impetus toward more cooperative relations with the Soviet Union was continued in the 1960s with increased trade between the former antagonists. In the 1970s this was supplemented with West Germany's *Ostpolitik*, American détente, and French efforts at forging special relations with the East in general and the Soviet Union in particular. These and many other initiatives by the other member of the alliance continued unabated through the decade and encouraged the perception, especially in Europe, of the peaceful intentions of the Soviet Union.[30] Additionally, Soviet political difficulties with its former satellites— Czechoslovakia, Rumania, Albania, and Poland—fostered the belief that the Soviets had more than enough to occupy themselves rather than initiate hostilities in Western Europe.

This reduced sense of threat occurred along with an increasing tendency of alliance members to obligate budgetary resources away from defense spending and more toward social welfare programs.[31] Increasing pressure from the political Left for greater government involvement in the amelioration of social conditions within the nations of the alliance was a major reason for the reallocation of the resources. The pressure for reduced defense spending was obviulsy reinforced by the decline in the sense of threat from the Soviet Union. The reduced defense spending also aided in the perpetuation of another situation. Because defense spending had been reduced and conventional forces were not maintained at former levels, the belief existed among many in NATO Europe that matching Soviet strength was not possible, even if it were politically desired.[32] Since NATO could not hope to match the Soviets in conventional forces, why should it try? Rather, NATO Europe was content to rely on the United States to provide for its ultimate security.

The divergence of views as to the purpose of NATO could clearly be seen in the debate surrounding the military strategy of the alliance. For NATO Europe, the overriding purpose of the

alliance was to deter the Soviet Union from attack by the threat
of an American strategic reprisal. For the United States, the overriding purpose of the alliance was to prevent Europe from being
occupied by the Soviet Union. Hence, NATO Europe favored a
military strategy which emphasized deterrence of an attack by the
Soviets through their fear of punishment by the American strategic missiles and bombs. The United States favored a strategy
which allowed it to deter the Soviets from attacking, yet denied
them military objectives if the attack did occur.

Given these divergent points of view on the purpose of the alliance and the proper focus of its military strategy, it was not
surprising that precision-guided munitions did not enjoy widespread acceptance within the alliance. The decline in their perception of a sense of threat by the Soviet Union, domestic pressures
for decreased military spending, and the desire not to be the site
of any battle—conventional or nuclear—have combined to orient
NATO Europe toward a military strategy of deterrence by punishment rather than by denial of objectives. To ensure that its favored military strategy existed de facto, NATO Europe was reluctant to partake of the new military technology, for to do so
would detract from its version of that strategy.

By increasing its conventional force capability, Europe feared
an increasing probability that NATO would be required to use it.
If NATO were capable of fighting a conventional war, then the
Soviets, who preferred to fight with conventional weapons to avoid
the dangers of escalation, would be encouraged to launch a conventional attack. That is, they would have been more encouraged
to do so than if NATO could only have responded briefly with
limited conventional forces and then resort to tactical nuclear
weapons, or surrender. By not developing its conventioanl force
capability and relying on tactical and strategic nuclear weapons as
deterrents, NATO Europe hoped to increase the deterrent capacity of the alliance.[33]

To extend this logic one step further, NATO opted for a poor
man's *force de frappe*. The French constructed the *force de frappe* in
great measure to assure nuclear weapons would be employed if
required in the event of war in Europe. To the French, this would
force the ultimate involvement of America's strategic missiles.

Cognizant of this, the Soviets would be deterred. Rather than opt for an expensive *force*, NATO Europe has sought to assure American use of nuclear weapons by virtue of Europe's weakness. In Thomas C. Schelling's analogy, it has burned its bridges behind it to ensure America has no choice but use of nuclear weapons.[34]

This logic was dictated by the individual needs of alliance members. They could not, for domestic political reasons, increase spending on defense, nor did their perception of the threat or their perspective on the proper NATO strategy dictate that they do so. Rather, NATO Europe was content to rely on American nuclear weapons to deter war. To ensure that those weapons would be used, Europe's apparent strategy was to remain weak in conventional forces. Therefore, precision-guided munitions did not and perhaps will not become substantially incorporated into the NATO alliance.

These predictions about the future of precision-guided munitions in the alliance and the reasons therefore are partly dependent upon circumstances remaining fairly static. Future changes in the international political system and in the domestic politics of the members of Europe may alter the validity of some of those conclusions. Let us turn now to an overall assessment of new technologies and NATO and attempt to predict how NATO might respond to future advances in weapon technologies.

NOTES

1. Henry A. Kissinger, *White House Years* (Boston: Little, Brown and Co., 1979), p. 83.

2. The Vladivostok Accord was identified as such by President Gerald Ford in November 1974.

3. As of this writing, the SALT II Treaty has been withdrawn from U.S. Senate consideration and its limitations were exceeded by the United States late in 1986. There is a possibility that Congressional action will force the Reagan administration to comply with the treaty limits.

4. U.S. Department of Defense, *Annual Report—Department of Defense, Fiscal Year 1980* (Washington, DC: 1979), p. 80, hereinafter cited as *DOD Annual Report, 1980*. The position of the window as of this writing is unclear. Recent American administration announcements regarding the

method of basing a new strategic missile (the MX) imply that "window" is closed. See Leslie H. Gelb, "As a Bargaining Chip, MX May Be No Bargain for the Soviets," *New York Times*, 24 April 1983, sec. 4, p. 1.

5. In the Alastair Buchan Memorial Lecture in 1977, German Chancellor Helmut Schmidt cautioned the other Western European states that "strategic arms limitations confined to the United States and the Soviet Union inevitably impair the security of Western European members of the Alliance vis-à-vis Soviet military superiority in Europe" unless the Alliance takes steps to reduce the conventional balance of forces in Europe. Again speaking of arms limitations, the Chancellor warned that "Europe must be particularly careful to insure [*sic*] that the negotiations do not neglect the components of NATO's deterrence strategy" and "to prevent any developments that could undermine the basis of this strategy." *Survival* 20 (January/February 1978): 2.

6. U.S. Department of Defense, *The Theater Nuclear Force Posture in Europe*, James R. Schlesinger, A Report to the U.S. Congress in compliance with Public Law 93-365 (Washington, DC: U.S. Government Printing Office, 1975), pp. 10–11, and *DOD Annual Report*, 1980, pp. 100–104.

7. U.S. Congress, Senate, Committee on Foreign Relations, Subcommittee on European Affairs, *SALT and the NATO Allies*, S. Rept. 96th Congress, 1st Session, 1979, pp. 5–7.

8. For example, prior to his meeting with Soviet President Leonid Brezhnev in 1980, French President Giscard d'Estaing is reported to have kept his intentions secret from Washington until a few hours before his departure for Moscow, *The Economist*, 24 May 1980, pp. 11–12. Although the foreign policy of present President Mitterand is more closely aligned to that of the United States, French independence persists.

9. In a toast to German Chancellor Helmut Schmidt, as reported in *The Economist*, 19 July 1980, p. 13.

10. The lack of a coordinated NATO response to Soviet pressure on Poland is significant. As was noted by American officials at the time, if NATO could not agree on the proper actions to be taken in response to trouble "in her own back yard," what could it agree upon?

11. In a speech by Richard Nixon on 15 March 1974. *Weekly Compilation of Presidential Documents: Richard Nixon* Vol. 10, 18 March 1974, p. 327.

12. "The Bonn Economic Summit," *The Economist*, 22 July 1978, p. 73.

13. As Robert W. Tucker, "America in Decline: The Foreign Policy of Maturity," *Foreign Affairs* 58 (April 1980): 450, noted, such policies "cannot but subject relations with Allies to constant strain."

14. Denmark was a most remarkable example of an alliance member

seeking individual accommodations with oil suppliers. Its 1980 contract
with Saudi Arabia gave that state the contractual right to suspend oil
delivery if the buyer (Denmark) "or any instrumentality thereof" con-
ducts itself "in such a manner as to bring the kingdom of Saudi Arabia
. . . into disrepute . . . in any manner whatsoever." Reported in *The
Economist* 21 May 1980, p. 91.

15. In those instances when increased resources were devoted to the
defense budgets of the individual NATO members, it was usually in support of non-NATO operations. Through the 1970s, the increases in defense spending during the decade by Great Britain, Greece, Turkey, Portugal, and the United States were largely in support of unilateral initiatives
in Northern Ireland, Cyprus, Angola, and Vietnam, respectively. The
remaining major contributor to forces levels in NATO was West Germany, which decreased the share of its Gross National Product devoted
to defense matters.

16. See Appendixes 3, 4, and 5 for the scope of U.S. development of
PGMs.

17. The microminiaturization of computer circuitry was especially
valuable in the development of cruise missiles. See "Long Range Cruise
Missiles," *Stockholm International Peace Research Institute (SIPRI) Yearbook,
1975* (Stockholm: 1975), chap. 11.

18. For example, France developed the ENTAC antitank missile in the
1950s, but did not pursue the technology in any other applications, and
did not significantly update it from the earliest efforts. See *Jane's Weapon
Systems*, 1976 (London: Jane's Yearbook, 1976).

19. See Appendixes 3, 4, and 5 for a listing of selected precision weapons and their country of development.

20. See n. 18 in chap. 7 for a sample of the writings on the issues.

21. Martin van Creveld, *Military Lessons of the Yom Kippur War: Historical Perspectives*, The Washington Press, No. 24 (Beverly Hills/London:
Sage Publications, 1975).

22. Steven Canby, "The Alliance and Europe: Part IV, Military Doctrine and Technology," *Adelphi Papers*, No. 109 (London: International
Institute for Strategic Studies, 1974–1975), and James Digby, "Precision-
Guided Weapons," *Adelphi Papers*, No. 118 (London: International Institute for Strategic Studies, 1975).

23. Canby, "The Alliance and Europe;" and in a reversal of his former
(1975) position, James Digby and Edison M. Cesar, Jr., "Utilization of
Modern Weapons Suitable for Europe" (Santa Monica, CA: Rand, 1978),
p. 115.

24. A typical example may be the new antitank guided missiles. These
precision-guided munitions replaced on a one-for-one basis the older ve-

hicle-mounted 106mm recoiless rifle as the primary antitank weapon of the infantry company. In some instances, the entire antitank guided missile assets of the battalion were consolidated and placed under battalion supervision. Despite this minor modification of the existing organizational structure, there were no additional missile sections added to the company.

25. A typical example of augmentation rather than replacement may be found in the shoulder fired surface-to-air weapon. This precision weapon was hailed as the replacement for the vehicle-mounted .50 caliber machine gun. However, new purposes for the vintage (World War II) .50 caliber have been found and it now coexists with the antitank missile. In this case, then, the overall logistical "tail" has been lengthened by the appearance of precision weaponry, since no weapon system was eliminated with its coming.

26. Harvey Ardman, "The Great 'Robot' Arms Race," *American Legion Magazine*, October 1972, p. 10.

27. Data on the status of the precision weaponry in NATO in the late 1970s are from U.S. Department of Defense, U.S. Concepts Analysis Agency, *Army Net Assessment of U.S./NATO and Soviet/Warsaw Pact Ground Combat Forces in Central Europe (1978–1984)* (Washington, DC: U.S. Dept. of Defense, Department of the Army, 1979), pp. 3–11; U.S. Department of Defense, Studies, Analysis and Gaming Agency, *Total Force Capability Assessment-80: Vol. II, Strategic Net Assessment of NATO and Warsaw Pact Worldwide and Regional Conventional Force Balance* (Washington, DC: U.S. Department of Defense, Organization of the Joint Chiefs of Staff, 1980), passim; and *Jane's Weapon Systems, 1980* (London: Jane's Yearbook, 1980), passim. The projections listed in the first two references for antitank guided missiles and surface-to-air guided missile densities in the force structures of the various NATO members in the mid 1980s have proved fairly accurate. See U.S. Department of Defense, U.S. Concepts Analysis Agency, *Army Force Planning Data and Assumptions FY85-94* (Washington, DC: U.S. Department of Defense, Department of the Army, 1984), pp. II-2-70 to 82, I-5-3, and II-5-72 to 74; and John M. Collins, *U.S.-Soviet Military Balance 1980–1985* (McClean, VA: Pergamon-Brassey's International Defense Publishers, 1985), pp. 205 and 224.

28. Ibid.

29. This is not to say that no changes to personnel strengths or logistics bases have occurred with precision weaponry. As discussed, some changes have occurred. However, the magnitude of these changes has been insignificant.

30. Changes in Europe's thinking about its role in NATO, American leadership, and Soviet intentions were widely reported. Europeans re-

mained committed to the alliance, but did not believe the nature of the threat warranted a dramatic increase in military spending. They wanted more evidence that America was attempting to reduce tensions and engage in arms control. They wanted a strong but not overwhelmingly armed America. An important segment of the population, however, dissented. The younger (28–35 years) university-educated group preferred neutrality over NATO, as opposed to older groups. See Stanley R. Sloan, "Crisis in NATO: A Problem in Leadership?" *NATO Review* 30 (August 1982): 13. See also n. 31.

31. Information on European changes in social values is from Ronald Inglehart, *The Silent Revolution* (Princeton: Princeton University Press, 1977), and Michael Howard, "Social Change and the Defense of the West," in *NATO: The Next Thirty Years*, ed. Kenneth A. Meyers (Boulder, CO: Westview Press, 1980), p. 345. See also, *World Opinion Update*, (May/June 1980): 77; 4 (July/August 1980): 99.

32. The problem of NATO perceiving the Soviets to be "ten feet tall," was first outlined in the 1960s when the United States was maneuvering to gain NATO approval of the strategy of "flexible response." It was resurrected by Robert W. Komer, "Treating NATO's Self-Inflicted Wound," *Foreign Policy* 13 (Winter 1973/1974): 34.

33. *Strategic Survey 1972* (London: International Institute for Strategic Studies, 1973), p. 19; and Irving Kristol, "NATO: The End of an Era," *Wall Street Journal*, 16 November 1973, p. 14.

34. Thomas C. Schelling, *Arms and Influence* (New Haven: Yale University Press, 1966), chap. 2.

9

Case Study Summary and Conclusions

New weapon technologies are frequently expected to perform a number of functions. New weapons which fly faster, dive deeper, or shoot more accurately are purported to possess great powers far beyond their technical characteristics. They are credited with being able to cause a reorganization of military forces, or change the manner in which warfare is fought, or preclude warfare altogether. But technology does not do these things; states do. While a new weapon technology may possess attractive performance characteristics, it does not by itself cause changes in the state system.

Previously, NATO military analysts have greeted the advent of new weapon technologies as the means to solve the military problems facing the alliance, thereby enhancing its cohesion and efficacy. This author has argued that such a relationship between technology and NATO is too simplistic to be accurate and, therefore, is misleading. There are factors other than the performance characteristics of a new technology that have shaped its effects on the alliance. The status of the international environment, ongoing, non-alliance related problems among its members, the nature of the technology and the extent and manner of its distribution within NATO have been argued by this author to be the significant factors which most shaped the overall effect of a new technology.

Using the above factors, this author has examined the advent of tactical nuclear weapons and precision-guided munitions (PGMs) to the NATO alliance. My purpose was to describe how NATO had responded to that new technology, and to analyze what effect it had on the alliance. Let us briefly summarize the major points of the case studies.

TACTICAL NUCLEAR WEAPONS CASE STUDY

The NATO alliance was formed during a period of clear American dominance of economic, political, and military power among the Western states. The United States had pledged its strategic nuclear capability to support NATO in a war against the Soviet Union, which then possessed formidable strength only in conventional military forces. Because of the clear nature of the Soviet threat, the weakness of Western Europe, and the overwhelming capacity of the United States, America set alliance policy for a unified and responsive NATO. As economic and security priorities challenged each other within the states of the alliance, the Eisenhower administration was anxious for the United States to retain its dominant position within Western Europe, but to reduce the economic costs of maintaining troops there. Therefore, it offered the new technology of tactical nuclear weapons to NATO as a firepower substitute for more costly manpower. Equally desirous of economic savings, NATO Europe supported the change. However, the United States maintained strict control of these weapons. Given the NATO policy of linkage between war in Europe and American strategic nuclear bombs, the United States continued to hold the key to European survival and thereby continued to set alliance policy.

With the advent of a Soviet tactical and strategic nuclear capability, the role of tactical nuclear weapons changed. Now feeling increasingly threatened by the linkage between tactical nuclear weapons in Europe and the vulnerability of its cities, the United States sought to revise NATO's strategy. But having substantially regained its economic and political health, NATO Europe sought an equal voice in the alteration of that strategy. For reasons of their own survival, NATO Europe and the United States each sought to have the other as the site of any future battlefield. With this division on the strategy of "flexible response" for their employment, tactical nuclear weapons came to symbolize the difference between the two parties and the unequal decision-making power of NATO members. It was NATO Europe's intention to deter the Soviet Union by the threat of rapid escalation from the use of tactical nuclear weapons to America's strategic might. Not wanting to risk war in Europe and its survival on the dubious threat of mutual destruction with the Soviet Union, the United States sought to deter war by minimizing the chances for Soviet success. Conventional forces were to be used to blunt Soviet advances, with tactical nuclear weapons to be used as a last resort, and as a means of intrawar deterrence within Continental Europe.

Rather than solve military problems within the alliance as had originally been forecast, tactical nuclear weapons have thus contributed to its political divisions. The weapons have provided a rationale for NATO Europe not to increase its conventional force levels, yet thereby ensured its military dependence on the United States. America used that dependence as a lever to force concessions, decreasing NATO's cohesion and efficacy.

PRECISION-GUIDED MUNITIONS CASE STUDY

In the second case study, the trends noted above continued unabated. The economies of Western Europe maintained their pace of development. Trade with the Soviet Union and its allies increased. Political initiatives with Eastern Europe proceeded, with Western Europe becoming increasingly concerned with American leadership within the Western community. Just as various states of Europe seemed to be developing political minds of their own, the United States appeared more concerned with its own interests than those of the alliance. The American involvement in Vietnam and the growth of Soviet strategic power were two major factors in drawing the focus of American attention away from NATO. Indeed, the American policy of détente was used as license for a similar European policy aimed at a rapprochement with the Soviet Union.

Within the alliance, problems described in the 1950s continued into the 1970s. Sensing a decline in the probability of a Soviet attack, burdened by increasing costs of social welfare programs, and desirous of continuing to reap the gains from trade with Soviet-bloc countries, Western Europe resented the strident American requests for greater European monetary and troop support for NATO-related activities. Various American hints at reduction of its troop levels in Europe without such support generated increased European concerns of American abandonment. European concern was also manifest about the increasing American emphasis on the war-fighting aspects of the strategy of "flexible response" coupled with the notion of the *non*-fighting aspects of Mutual Assured Destruction. This concern was reinforced by America's closely guarded bilateral negotiations with the Soviet Union on strategic arms and by the growth of those same Soviet strategic arms. Aware of Europe's concern, the United States was content to repeat its assurances of strategic support, which sounded hollow in view of the Soviet's strategic power. Despite their seemingly incredible nature, Europeans used these assurances as the rationale not to maintain conventional force levels, further weakening the notion of any "flexible response."

The debates over "flexible response" and the requirements generated by alliance policies usually turned on the matter of economics. In the early 1970s, precision-guided munitions were hailed as an expensive new technology that would allow alliance members to acquire the capability needed to implement NATO strategy. The new technology was accurate, non-nuclear, low cost, and widely available, which seemingly made it ideally suited for incorporation into NATO. But despite their seeming attractiveness, PGMs did not live up to their advance billing. A decade after their appearance, these weapons had become prisoner to other factors.

By the end of the decade, the Soviet Union had achieved a clear parity in strategic weapons and a superiority in many areas of conventional weapons. Cognizant of American-Soviet strategic parity, several European members of NATO continued their policies of rapprochement with the Eastern European states, and tension levels between the European members of the two blocs remained low. More than its alliance partners, the United States was concerned about Soviet intentions in the wake of occasional crises in the Middle East, Southeast Asia, Africa, and Soviet military build up.

Within NATO Europe, there was uneven acceptance of precision weapons as its members cited fiscal restraints, détente, and the overwhelming Soviet strength as reasons for not building their conventional forces. In fact, that reluctance stemmed from a divergence on military strategy springing from a nagging doubt about American credibility. Rather than maintain the conventional capability required by the concept of "flexible response," NATO Europe was more desirous of creating conditions to force inflexibly an early American decision to resort to nuclear weapons in order to deter the initial attack. The United States was equally desirous of avoiding those conditions and sought vainly to encourage development of NATO's conventional war-fighting capacity.

Thus, the reluctance to capitalize upon the obvious military benefits provided by precision weaponry was due to a divergence of views on alliance strategy fueled by doubts of American credibility and compounded by domestic politics and differing perceptions of the threat. Rather than contribute to the resolution of the alliance's conventional military ills, PGMs served to foster alliance divisions and crystallize the military dependence of NATO Europe upon America.

CONCLUSIONS

These studies of the advent of new weapon technology to NATO allow us to draw several conclusions about the effects of these new technologies on the alliance. The conclusions are discussed separately below.

• The possession of superior military power is the basis for dominance in the setting of alliance policy. As the possessor of superior military power in the early days of NATO, the United States was able to shape the structure and operational policy of the alliance to suit its needs. However, as American needs changed, as with the "New Look" of 1953 and "flexible response" in 1961, so did the operating policy. European members of NATO were unable to block completely this latest change, even though they recognized the possibility of it being deleterious to their interests.

With the development of Soviet strategies and military power in the 1970s, however, the calculus of policy making ability shifted. This growth in Soviet nuclear power acted as a counterpoise in that power vis-à-vis NATO Europe and, consequently in the ability of the United States to set alliance policy. The debate in the early 1980s over Intermediate Nuclear Forces is instructive. The United States awaited European acceptance of installation there of its proposed modernized theater nuclear capability while being forced by NATO Europe to pursue arms control talks for reduction of those weapons.

From this conclusion, it would follow that in the event a new weapon technology were to be developed that would grant the possessor superior usable military power within NATO, it would not, however, confer on its owner the ability to set alliance policy. This would suggest that, although several alliance members are capable of developing such a new weapon technology, only a slim possibility exists for NATO to acquire a new dominant actor to replace the United States. France, Germany, and Great Britain, in that order, are the most likely candidates to supplant the United States as the alliance leader, because of the advanced status of their technological development relative to other members of NATO. This is not to say that some member(s) of NATO might not rise to prominence within the alliance. This possibility will be discussed in chapter 10.

The designation of military power as the basis for dominance in setting alliance policy is due to the nature of the alliance. As a military coalition, the basis for dominance is military capability; power based on the other sources was not a sufficient "ante" for the game. For example, although Europe had regained a large measure of its economic capacity by the 1960s, there was no indication that this relative redistribution of economic power vis-à-vis the United States was able to be converted into leverage in shaping alliance policy, although it did foster strains within the alliance.[1] Recall that in the early 1960s, NATO Europe was unable to persuade the United States to relinquish control of any of its nuclear weapons during the conceptual development of the

Multi-Lateral Force. Hence, the concept was stillborn. However, in 1961, the United States announced its own strategic policy of "flexible response" which was widely perceived as being counter to European interests. In the intervening six years, NATO Europe (notably Great Britain and West Germany) did have some success in having that policy modified to gloss over important divergent views about that policy. The policy and those divergent views continue today.

• Rather than meet the military requirements of NATO and enhance its cohesion and efficacy, new weapon technologies are more likely to be the catalyst by which divergences become manifest. That is, new weapon technologies may produce the opposite effects expected by military analysts or proponents. Tactical nuclear weapons were sought by NATO as a substitute for economically and socially expensive manpower. They were to allow the alliance to use the firepower of nuclear technology to substitute for the manpower judged impossible to obtain. But rather than providing the means for meeting the alliance's military requirements and thereby enhancing its efficacy, tactical nuclear weapons soon became the focus for debate on NATO strategy. The development by the Soviet Union of its own tactical nuclear weapons and strategic nuclear capability lay bare the absolute dependence of NATO Europe on the strategic guarantee of the United States. Tactical nuclear weapons, which were to be the saving substitute for manpower, had become at the same time the devices that would quickly and inevitably force America's resort to its strategic power in the event of war in Europe (against American wishes) or allow the war, if it came, to be fought in a limited manner on European soil (against European wishes). The debate engendered by these divergent perspectives is not likely to end soon.

Precision-guided munitions became a victim of the same phenomenon as tactical nuclear weapons. Hailed as an inexpensive substitute of firepower for manpower, this new technology was to offset the large Warsaw Pact superiority in manpower, tanks, and aircraft. But rather than pursue this new technology, the European members were more concerned about strengthening the linkage to America's strategic weapons. Equally concerned that it might be asked to honor its strategic guarantee, the United

States pursued this new weapon technology in order to enhance NATO's conventional capability, while at the same time exhorted its allies to do more militarily.

• New weapon technologies are not likely to be readily accepted by NATO. This flows logically from the previous conclusion. Regardless of its classification as nuclear or non-nuclear, a new weapon technology is not likely to be readily accepted by NATO under the present circumstances. In the case of nuclear weapons, the case study revealed that the Americans had been extremely reluctant to share the technical knowledge and control of the employment of nuclear weapons. If a new weapon technology were to be developed which involved nuclear explosive or propulsive power, the possessor would likely offer that technology to NATO only in a very restricted sense, such as has occurred in the past. France, Great Britain, and the United States have all, for various reasons, kept the secrets and control of their respective nuclear technologies to themselves. Because of the unknowns involved in the enlarged circle of members of the "nuclear club," it is likely that the control of a new nuclear technology would not be made available to the general membership of NATO. Additionally, it is not clear that other NATO states desire nuclear weapon technology. The Benelux countries, particularly Luxemburg, are extremely reluctant to allow nuclear weapons on their soil, as are Norway, Iceland, Portugal, and Spain. West Germany's admittance to NATO in 1955 was predicated on the fact that it would not seek to develop nuclear weapons; public opinion polls in West Germany indicate continuing opposition to that development. The Non-Proliferation Treaty, signed by all members of the alliance except France and Spain, is another factor which would preclude widespread dispersion of new nuclear technology within NATO. In sum, new nuclear technology is not likely to be widespread within NATO because the possessors are not desirous of expanding the membership in the "nuclear club" and because serious political and social obstacles exist to its adoption in the non-nuclear states of NATO.

If NATO is not likely to adopt new nuclear weapon technology, neither is it likely to accept a new weapon technology of a conventional nature. A new conventional technology will likely create the conditions which NATO seeks to avoid: a conventional war that is "winable" or has a "winner" is a war that is more likely to be fought than one that has only "losers." NATO Europe is caught in the predicament of requiring sufficient conventional military forces to preclude a relatively unopposed "quick grab" by the Soviets, yet not so many forces as to make the resort to nuclear weapons appear unlikely. To draw a weak analogy from the strategic balance for NATO Europe, a delicate balance between inadequacy and sufficiency is required in conventional weaponry. New technology that appears to upset that balance in the direction of enhanced conventional capability is not likely to be readily accepted.

The lack of support for new weapon technologies by most NATO members is understandable from an economic perspective as well. One would not expect the smaller members of the alliance to expend proportionately large economic resources to produce in return only a marginally slight increase in NATO's deterrent capability, and such has been the case. Only the economically stronger states of the alliance have pursued new weapon technologies. The United States, France, and Great Britain pursued the development of tactical nuclear weapons, and those states plus Germany and Italy became the major possessors of precision weaponry.

• The external threat to NATO will be the determining factor in the acceptance of new weapon technology. In the early 1950s, the Soviet threat was perceived by NATO to be sufficient to warrant the fielding of ninety-six divisions. Such a goal was almost immediately judged infeasible by those very same members and the more economic substitute of a new weapon technology was sought. In response to the external threat, tactical nuclear weapons were accepted by NATO members as a means of providing the divisions' equivalent in firepower. Although the new weapon technology was retained largely under the control of the United States, the offer of the weapons and the strategy for their employment were rapidly accepted by NATO members, thereby enhancing alliance unity.

In the second case study, with the decline in the sense of Soviet threat by NATO Europe, the readiness to accept the new precision munitions technology was generally low, despite American pressure to do so. Despite the technology's attractive properties of widespread availability, cost-effectiveness, and low cost, there was not general movement within the alliance to embrace this new technology. Relative to NATO Europe, the United States sensed a greater threat to Europe from the Soviet Union and sought this new technology, but on a scale much reduced from that envisioned earlier by military analysts.

The Soviet Union is also capable of producing the new precision munitions technology, and has fielded a number of antitank and antiaircraft precision munitions. In the event the Soviet Union further equips its forces, and NATO uniformly senses a threat, NATO may feel compelled to accept the new precision munition technology more as a matter of self-defense—again in response to a sense of threat. However, before the unlikely event of NATO Europe developing an increasing sense of threat from the Soviet Union, other fundamental changes in the structure of the alliance are likely to have occurred. These changes are as a result of the aforementioned growth of Soviet strategic power, in the increased economic and political independence of NATO Europe from the United States, and the perceived requirements of an American global foreign policy. These changes to the structure of NATO and the implications for new weapon technologies will be discussed in the concluding chapter.

CONFIRMATION OF THE FRAMEWORK

In most instances, these observations support the conceptual framework developed in the initial chapter. To recapitulate that framework briefly, it was posited that there existed a number of variables which would affect the manner in which NATO responded to the introduction of new weapon technology. The structure and the nature of the distribution of power within the international political system were such variables in the environment of NATO. Within NATO, the governing structure, the operational military doctrine, and the general level of cohesion and efficacy were factors which were influenced by the environment and would be affected by the new weapon technology. Finally, this author posited that the nature of the new weapon technology itself would aslo influence its effect on NATO.

The case studies confirmed that the environment of NATO does have an effect on its functioning and its acceptance of new weapons technologies. The alliance was itself created in response to a sense of Soviet threat in the bipolar era of the 1940s. Political divisions, which developed from time to time within NATO, were overcome by periodic resurgences in the perceived severity of the threat by the Soviets. Conflicts over such issues as German rearmament, force size, and composition, and the distribution of the financial burden of the alliance were overcome by crises with the Soviet Union over Berlin, the Korean invasion, and Hungary. But as fears of that threat declined, particularly in the European states, and as the dangers of general nuclear war became more apparent to NATO and the Warsaw Pact, the frequency and severity of the crises declined. Without the universally perceived specter of the Soviet threat to provide the amalgam for the alliance, and lacking a clear substitute to soothe its divisions, NATO's difficulties continued and its cohesion suffered. As another factor in the environment of NATO, the declining economic dominance of the United States over Western Europe in the early 1960s did not translate into a decline of its dominance in the military affairs of NATO. The United States remained able, with little difficulty, to resist demands for a share in the decision-making authority over the release of nuclear weapons and the setting of alliance policy in general. Indeed, it instituted a strategy within the alliance which required tight control over those weapons. In this instance, extra-alliance symmetrical economic power relationships were not able to be translated into political leverage within the alliance. However, with the arrival of mulipolarity in the international system and the condition of strategic parity between the United States and the Soviet Union in the 1970s, alliance unity and America's ability to dominate policy making within NATO had eroded. The relative balance of its strategic power by an external agent—the Soviet Union—had decreased the dominance of the policy-making ability of the United States within the alliance.

The structural apparatus of NATO had an effect on the manner in which the technology was incorporated. In the case of tactical nuclear weapons, the requirement for unanimous approval of a policy before implementing it, and the physical possession of the vast majority of the tactical nuclear weapons held by the members of NATO assured the United States of control over the employment of that new technology. Desiring to maintain authority for the decision to employ tactical nuclear weapons, the United States could veto any policy which threatened the control of tactical nuclear weapons and remain completely within the strictures of the NATO Treaty. It was this ability to control the release of tactical nuclear weapons and hence affect the linkage to America's strategic weapons which was largely responsible for the departure of France from the military structure of NATO. With the case of precision munitions, the structure of the alliance also provided NATO Europe the ability to resist American encouragement to increase its conventional force capability. Just as the United States could resist European demands for a shared control over nuclear weapons, so too could Europe resist the United States on matters of conventional forces. Just as easily, Europe was able to resist American pressure on issues deemed unrelated to NATO.[2]

The cohesion of the alliance was not affected by the new technology qua technology. Rather, its effect on alliance cohesion was due to the political perceptions created by the prospect of its incorporation. Tactical nuclear weapons and precision weapons demonstrably had certain physical characteristics which had military application. However, these characteristics also had political implications which were far more important than whatever military benefit the weapons may be thought to have provided to NATO. Most importantly, it was those political implications which were instrumental in determining how the alliance responded to the new technology.

The compatibility of the new technology with current alliance doctrine appears to have been unimportant. In both case studies, the new technology was compatible with the current doctrine, yet the technology was accepted in one case but not in the other. Demonstrated most clearly in the precision munitions case study, the strategy itself was the reason for any debate on new weapon technology—not the technology.

In summary, in most respects the generalized framework developed in the introduction to this study has been found accurate to analyze the critical factors which determined the outcome of the introduction of two new weapon technologies into NATO. Among the different factors, the role of the environment is judged to have been the most critical, and the nature of the new technology the least important. The salience of the threat and the military capability of the Soviet Union appears to be the key factor which has influenced the degree of acceptance of the new weapon technologies. When the threat of Soviet aggression into the NATO area appeared high, and the Soviet military capacity to degrade the credibility of the strategic guarantee of the United States was low, the new weapon technology was readily accepted by NATO. As those conditions changed, so has the attitude of NATO Europe about new weapon technology. With NATO Europe's perception of a diminished Soviet threat and its great concern about the reliability of the American strategic pledge, the reluctance of NATO to pursue widespread employment of the new precision weapon technology was evident. And it does not appear that the nature of the new weapon technology would have made an appreciable difference in the manner or degree of its acceptance. Whether nuclear or non-nuclear, expensive or low cost, widely available or relatively closely controlled, any new weapon technology is not likely to be widely accepted by the European members of NATO. Rather than be accepted by the alliance, the new weapon technology is more likely to become the vehicle for divisive debate within NATO, thereby reinforcing its divisions and increasing disunity.

Armed with this information, it is possible to foresee more confidently the effects of other new technologies which may soon be offered to NATO. Since there are certain methodological dangers in attempting to predict future relationships based on the observation of two past events, caution is indeed warranted. Also, there is some danger in believing that conditions present in the NATO alliance and its environment when the full effects of tactical nuclear weapons and precision weapons became clear will remain present in the future. For the moment, let us assume that is the case and select a new weapon technology that is similar to that already studied. The Enhanced Radiation weapon, or the "neutron bomb" as it has been popularly known, is another new technology weapon that has been touted as a great aid in the solution of NATO's military ills. What is this new weapon and what can the observations from the previous case studies tell us about the likely effect of this new technology? What problems can be foreseen, and can they be obviated?

NEUTRON BOMB—OLD WINE
IN A NEW BOTTLE?

In the past few years, there has been substantial discussion about a new nuclear technology that is "more humane." The Enhanced Radiation, or neutron bomb, weapon has been hailed by its proponents as an effective battlefield weapon which will offset the increasing Soviet/Warsaw Pact advantage in tanks, but will do so with vastly less collateral damage than is possible using present nuclear weapons. Opponents of the new weapon are many and divided. Some feel that resources could be better spent on other, more accurate conventional weapons (such as PGMs) which would also defeat the tank threat, but without the risks of nuclear war. Other opponents are concerned that neutron weapons will induce a lowering of the nuclear threshold and the likelihood of war itself by making war more fightable, and hence more likely to be fought. Still others reject the notion that more weapons, especially nuclear weapons, will make NATO more secure.

As has been noted, the objective physical characteristics of new weapon technologies are less important factors that the subjective perception of those characteristics. But some knowledge of those characteristics is needed in order to understand the starting points for the debate which has arisen. A brief description of this new technology will highlight the salient features which will be valuable in a discussion of its possible future in NATO.

All nuclear explosions produce four effects: blast, heat, residual radiation ("fallout"), and prompt radiation.[3] Prompt radiation consists mostly of invisible, highly penetrating neutrons. A typical standard fission explosion such as is produced by current tactical nuclear weapons will generate its effects in following proportions: blast—50 percent, heat—35 percent, fallout—10 percent, and initial nuclear radiation—5 percent. The neutron bomb uses a different detonation process in order to reallocate the distribution of those effects. It produces vastly increased amounts of neutrons, but with greatly reduced blast and heat effects. The lethality of such an enhanced radiation weapon accrues principally from the effects of neutron irradiation, which causes a breakdown of some of the constituents essential to normal body cell functioning.

With its redistribution of energy emissions, the blast effect of an enhanced radiation weapon will cover an area approximately one-tenth of that of a standard fission weapon ten times its yield. But the prompt radiation produced by the enhanced radiation weapon will cover the same area as the blast effect of the standard fission weapon. That is, the lethality effects of the enhanced radiation weapon cover an equal area, but with substantially less blast effect than a standard fission weapon.

Explosions from enhanced radiation weapons have the same bright flash, radiation emission, and mushroom-shaped cloud of a standard fission weapon. Within NATO, the United States is the leading developer of this new technology and will make neither the technology nor the physical control of these weapons available to other alliance members. The French are also pursuing the development of the neutron bomb, but are less advanced than the United States, which has begun production but not deployment of these weapons.[4]

THE FRAMEWORK AND THE NEUTRON BOMB

Given these performance characteristics, how does NATO perceive this new technology, and how is it likely to react to American efforts to incorporate it into the alliance? Using the knowledge gained from the study of tactical nuclear and precision weapons, how might potential problems be obviated?

The observations derived from the two case studies can be summarized as follows:

- The external threat to NATO will be the decisive factor in determining the acceptance of new weapon technology.
- New weapon technologies are not likely to be accepted by NATO on the basis of their performance characteristics.
- Rather than enhance its cohesion by solving NATO's military problems, new weapon technologies are more likely to become catalysts for divisive debate within NATO, before and/or after their adoption.
- The possession of dominant military power within NATO pro-

vided the United States with the basis for dominance of NATO
policy making.

   Taking these observations in reverse order, the growth of Soviet strategic military power has effectively counterbalanced that
of the United States and, in the process, decreased the ability of
the United States to set policy within NATO. The new military
technology represented by the neutron bomb will not fundamentally change that balance. Because the Warsaw Pact forces possess
almost three times as many tanks as do NATO forces, the neutron bomb is not likely to offer the United States a military advantage over the Soviet Union, but at best would provide the
means to reduce the Soviet's advantage.[5] This rearrangement of
the tank forces imbalance would not be sufficient to allow the
United States to resume its former position of dominance within
the alliance.
   Symptomatic of this American loss of political dominance within
the alliance would be the divisive debate that would likely arise if
the United States were to attempt to coerce NATO diplomatically
into acceptance of the neutron bomb.[6] Rather than being a partial
solution to the problem of the military tank force imbalance and,
hence, a device to increase its cohesion and efficacy, an attempt to
introduce the neutron bomb into NATO would most likely cause
debate at least equal to that generated by the Intermediate Nuclear
Force modernization effort. The neutron bomb has been identified
by NATO Europe as a war-fighting weapon and, therefore, as a
device to make war more likely to occur.[7] Additionally, the argument has been raised in Europe that the neutron bomb, far from
causing less collateral damage, would likely result in an increased
amount of damage, since it is likely to be employed in a nondis-
criminating manner.[8] The counter arguments of the weapon's
proponents are well known from the previous discussions on
NATO strategy and need not be repeated.[9] The essential point
here is that, far from providing the basis for alliance cohesion and
efficacy, attempts to introduce the neutron bomb into NATO will
likely be dysfunctional.
   That debate on the neutron bomb would likely bring about the
conditions envisioned by the next conclusion of our case studies:
the new weapon technology is not likely to be adopted by NATO,

regardless of the weapon's performance characteristics or the expressed military "need" within the alliance. A large-scale debate generated by the neutron bomb is one that is certain to lay bare the divisions and inconsistencies of the present alliance relationships. Lacking the ability to coerce diplomatically the members of NATO as it has previously, the United States already has seen efforts to introduce the neutron bomb as doomed. The long-festering issues of American control of the nuclear trigger and flexible options for the defense of Europe have created irreversible concerns about American willingness to employ nuclear weapons. At the same time there exists concern that America will abandon Europe to the fate of a theater war in hopes of preserving its own territory, or that America will readily use the neutron bomb to battle the Soviets in an attempt to deter further war—again confining the conflict to war in Europe. Desirous of avoiding these extremes, it is likely that NATO will be content with the weaponry that has apparently deterred the Soviets in the past, and will seek to avoid the unknown danger posed by this new technology.

This condition is even more certain to exist if the fundamental trends existent within NATO continue unabated. The divergences in the sense of threat from the Soviet Union perceived by the various members of NATO continue to affect their judgments in matters of foreign policy. Led by its smaller states, the members of NATO perceive Soviet incentives to use military power as substantially less than the degree perceived by the United States, and especially by the Reagan administration. There is therefore an even greater likelihood that NATO Europe will continue to reject the new weapon technology. The asymmetrical sense of threat from the Soviet Union has fostered two different, yet converging, political views, either alone capable of causing the rejection of the neutron bomb by NATO. The decreased sense of Soviet threat felt by the governments of Europe has made those governments reluctant to engage in military enhancement programs for two reasons. First, the programs are not needed since the threat is not deemed sufficient to warrant such actions, and, second, those governments are desirous of avoiding provocative actions which would touch off a round of conventional and nuclear arms production by the Soviets. Clearly, this reluctance to chance the provocation of a new arms buildup would be fueled by adept

Soviet propaganda efforts, much as occurred with the Intermediate Nuclear Force issue.

On the other hand, the continuance of the American predilection to find the Soviet "invisible hand" at the root of every international problem and the tendency to see the primary threat from the Soviet Union as a military one which requires force to match force are reasons which have encouraged the growth in Europe of increasingly vocal elements of left-oriented parties which call for a fundamental reappraisal of NATO and their country's approach to it. Given the fragile nature of the governing coalitions/slender majorities of most of the states of NATO and the magnitude of the other problems (principally economic) that they face, the governments of NATO Europe will continue to be very reluctant to venture into the unknown waters surrounding the adoption of the neutron bomb.

What, then, lies ahead for the neutron bomb? If alliance problems of cohesion and efficacy are politically motivated, they will not be solved by technology, but by politics. One such political solution to the problem of the neutron bomb and NATO would be to seek to use this new technology as a "bargaining chip" to obtain Soviet military concessions. Rather than seek a military or technological counter to the growth of Soviet power which at the same time would be counterproductive to the alliance, America could seek a political solution that has less alliance-wrenching potential. To be sure, there are some dangers in this course of action. "Bargaining chips" have a way of taking on a life of their own, and thus there is no certainty that use of the neutron bomb as a means to extract diplomatic concessions from the Soviets would not have negative consequences for NATO. But only rarely is there such certainty present in matters of interstate relations.

However, the prospect for obtaining meaningful concessions from the Soviet Union for striking some bargain on the neutron bomb is judged to be quite remote. The reason is simple: the Soviets are not likely to bargain away any of their existing systems on the promise that NATO will give up something that it cannot agree to deploy. Every American president since Kennedy has had the same observation about bargaining with the Soviets: they don't listen to what you say; they watch what you do. If the members of NATO will not agree to allow the stationing of the neutron bomb on their soil, much less agree to the integration of that weapon into operational war plans, then the Soviets are not likely to want to pay any price to ensure its non-deployment. As such, the future of the neutron bomb looks particularly bleak: remaining in partially-assembled storage in the United States.

In many ways, however, the problems associated with the attempt at deployment of the neutron bomb are relatively minor. Since the 1978 reversal of its deployment policy, controversy over that new technology has largely subsided and certainly has been overshadowed by other events such as Soviet troops in Afghanistan, the natural gas pipeline deal between Central European states and the Soviets, the Falklands war, American aid to rebel forces in Nicaragua, and terrorism and counterterrorism activities by a variety of states. Indeed, NATO seems doomed to career wildly from one crisis to another, never quite resolving one episode while it races breathlessly toward the next controversy, yet somehow always surviving more or less intact. While such "success" is to be admired, it may not be the best way to do business, and the string of "successes" may run out. A particularly thorny issue involving an emerging new weapon technology has provided the latest threat to that string. The Strategic Defense Initiative program begun by the United States has raised again many of the divisions within the alliance and promises to become the defense issue of the decade. This space-based, antiballistic missile system has been billed as a means of making obsolete all nuclear weapons and therefore, presumably, nuclear war. What is this new technology? Is it indeed likely to end nuclear war? How will it be received by NATO? By applying the results of our study of past new weapon technologies we can offer insights into the likely future of this technology and offer some suggestions to minimize its anticipated negative effects on NATO.

NOTES

1. The reason for this inability to translate economic power into political power within NATO was because EEC members were unable to agree about anything more than mutually advantageous reductions of barriers to trade and were unable to develop formal decision-making

structures to focus on political problems. This inability to agree on political matters may increase as additional, disparate members are added to
the EEC. On the other hand, within the last few years, Europe has made
surprising progress toward integration. This topic will be addressed in
the final chapter.

   2. Examples of recent European reluctance to support actively the policies of the United States as regards Soviet activities would include the
Soviet invasion of Afghanistan and the attendant U.S.-sponsored sanctions, U.S. policy toward Nicaragua and El Salvador, the natural gas
pipeline deal, and the Polish situation.

   3. Much of the discussion on the physical characteristics and functioning of the neutron bomb is from information provided directly to the
author by letter from the Defense Nuclear Agency, 28 April 1978, and
from Congressional Research Service, "Enhanced Radiation Weapons: 'The
Neutron Bomb,' " (Washington, DC: Library of Congress, 1979).

   4. France has developed a neutron bomb and has tested the bomb successfully. Its deployment status is not clear at this time, although it may
be presumed to be proceeding.

   5. International Institute for Strategic Studies, *The Military Balance 1981–
1982* (London: International Institute for Strategic Studies, 1981), p. 125.

   6. While European attitudes about the neutron bomb have been a matter of record, the United States apparently still harbors the belief that the
neutron bomb can be deployed to Europe. Reagan administration spokesmen have recently mentioned the possibility of merely deploying the
neutron bomb without ascertaining European permission.

   7. Although agreed upon initially for deployment to Europe, resent-
ment of the weapon continues, especially after the American "flip-flop"
on the issue in 1978. See Eliot A. Cohen, "The Long-Term Crisis of the
Alliance," *Foreign Affairs* 61 (Winter 1982/83): 339.

   8. One American proponent of the neutron bomb (who was a member
of the Reagan administration transition team) blithely suggests that the
weapon be used to "flush" the enemy from suspected locations during
war in Europe. See S. T. Cohen, *The Neutron Bomb: Political, Technological, and Military Issues* (Cambridge, MA: Institute for Foreign Policy
Analysis, Inc., 1978), pp. 70–71.

   9. Among military analysts, some proponents of the Enhanced Radia-
tion Warhead are: Daniel Gans, "Neutron Weapons: Solution to a Sur-
prise Attack," *Military Review* 62 (January 1982): 19; Kent F. Wisner,
"Military Aspects of Enhanced Radiation Weapons," *Survival* 23
(Nov./Dec. 1981): 246; Alex Vardamis, "The Neutron Warhead: Stormy
Past, Uncertain Future," *Parameters* 8 (March 1978): 40; and S. T. Cohen,
The Neutron Bomb.

10

Strategic Defense Initiative—The New Technology of the Decade

In March 1983, during a televised address to the American people, President Ronald Reagan announced his vision of a world free from reliance on nuclear weaponry.[1] In very brief terms near the end of his speech, the American president announced his intention to scrap the present system of nuclear deterrence, which he deemed "immoral and obsolete." While some administration spokesmen have since acknowledged that the president may have been too optimistic, the announcement did set in motion a variety of processes that have developed an increasing degree of momentum. Debates about the degree of "leakage" achievable or necessary, the desirability of "smart rocks" versus chemical lasers, the effect of the research on present and future arms control agreements, the morality of a concept which explicitly employs nuclear weapons for defensive purposes, and the effect of such a program on an already soaring federal budget deficit promise to make the proposal for a Strategic Defense Initiative (SDI) a permanent feature of the American political scene for some time.

Although the SDI has the potential for a fundamental revision of a large section of the political-military landscape, this discussion will concentrate on its potential consequences for the NATO alliance. Using the observations gleaned from the manner in which NATO responded to the introduction of previous instances of new weapon technologies, I will outline the pitfalls which appear to be involved in the introduction of this latest bit of technology. Finally, I will offer some suggestions on avoiding those pitfalls and some observations about the likely future of the alliance. Before commencing these discussions, let us briefly examine the technology to bring into sharper focus the reason for the widespread and increasingly strident nature of the debates.

THE TECHNOLOGY

The SDI as orginally unveiled was greeted with some skepticism, and identified by some pundits as an "afterthought" the president had appended to a speech on the budget he had just submitted to the Congress for consideration. Whatever the length of its gestation period, the SDI has certain characteristics which qualify it as a future new weapon technology and, as such, bestow upon it the potential for a fundamental alteration of the manner in which political-military affairs in NATO are conducted. Although all the elements of the system are in various stages of research and development, the general outlines of the technology are fairly clear. Since the primary focus of this discussion is not technical in nature, the present degree of uncertainty regarding the final characteristics of the technology does not preclude a discussion of its political ramifications. For both reasons, only a brief discussion of the technologies will follow.

The Strategic Defense Initiative proposed by the Reagan administration has been accused of many things, due mainly to two competing versions of the program set forth by elements of the administration. President Reagan and, to a lesser extent, Secretary of Defense Weinberger, have described the proposal as a means to make nuclear weapons obsolete; others have taken a more cautious view of its potential. The Reagan/Weinberger view of a world without nuclear weapons seems much too optimistic a reading of SDI's potential. In the absence of a companion series of sweeping arms control agreements, there does not appear to this author to be much chance of such a future. Additionally, there are other things, as of this writing, that it is not. It is *not* a weapons system awaiting deployment and it is not a deus ex machina that will confer world peace. It *is* a proposal for research in this and the next decade to determine if it is feasible to pursue weapon technologies that in the next millennium will reduce reliance on offensive systems as the means to ensure their non-use, and will reduce the threat to civilian population centers. Both of these goals are possible only if the SDI is accompanied by arms control agreements which limit offensive strategic nuclear systems. Let us sketch the outlines of each of these three elements of SDI.

First, the Reagan administration's call for the SDI was one to encourage the exploration of a variety of emerging technologies to determine their feasibility and suitability as components of a complex system of defense of the American homeland against ballistic missiles. Costing about $26 billion over some five to six years, the initial phase of the SDI program was designed to answer a series of basic engineering and scientific questions that must be addressed before the promise of these emerging technologies can be fully assessed.[2] The technologies being investigated in the SDI program will combine to offer a "layered" defense—that is, a defense that would use a variety of techniques to destroy or disable attacking missiles during various phases of thier flight.[3] "Layers" and their associated technologies presently under study would address the boost phase, the post-boost phase, and the terminal or reentry phase of the missiles' flight.

The boost phase is that period shortly after the missile is launched. During this phase, enemy missiles would be attacked by either ground or space-based chemical or X-ray lasers which would project a beam of energy (off a space-based mirror for ground-based lasers) toward the boost vehicle in order to burn through either the guidance section or the rocket motor bottle, rendering the missile inoperable.

In the post-boost phase, the warhead bus or vehicle which sits atop the missile and disperses warheads during the latter portion of the trajectory would be attacked. Again, during this phase chemical or X-ray–induced laser energy from space-based weapons would be used to burn through critical missile components. Alternatively, the bus might be vulnerable to attack by kinetic energy "rail guns" employing electromagnetic fields to accelerate and launch "smart" projectiles (terminally-guided projectiles using on-board homing sensors) to home in on the warhead bus and destroy it by either exploding nearby or actually striking the bus. Those warheads that were released from the warhead bus would travel for some tens of minutes in space and would continue to be vulnerable to attack by the laser weapons, or the "rail gun" technology.

During the terminal or reentry phase of flight as the surviving number of warheads approached their targets, they would come under attack by ground-based interceptors using conventional rocket technology and either nuclear or conventional explosive charges. This technology is probably the most developed of any of the aforementioned techniques, since programs for its use have continued apace despite the American decision in 1974 to dismantle its ABM complex in North Dakota.

To detect and track enemy missiles, and to control this complicated system of layered defenses, some integrated computer system would be required to detect a missile launch, determine its proportions and destination, track the missiles, alert and control the firing of the various systems involved in the several phases of the defensive network, and identify surviving missiles for subsequent attack. Obviously, this is a difficult task and even more difficult to "debug" the computer systems. Too, countermeasures could and would be taken by the attacker to outwit the system or complicate its job or overwhelm its capabilities. Chaff dropped from missiles could confuse space-based radars; multiple, lightweight decoys could be used to overload the targeting system; and protective coatings could be applied to missile components to foil laser–burning attempts. Perhaps most critically, the communications network required to control the space-base systems could be blinded or degraded by a variety of interference techniques, resulting in "decapitation" of the entire system. This is just a small flavoring of the obstacles that are being considered in research to deploy an effective system. In the course of weapons development, surely additional, perhaps insoluble, problems will be encountered.

STRATEGIC IMPLICATIONS OF THE SDI

The administration at present is calling for only a preliminary research effort to explore the feasibility of the SDI. However, in proposing the program, the administration has made it clear that, if deployed, this defensive system will alter the manner in which we have historically conceived of strategic deterrence. Rather than not defending our population centers (either with antiballistic missile sites, or passively with civil defense programs) to demonstrate our unwillingness to launch a first strike against the Soviet Union (thereby inviting a retaliatory blow against our undefended cities), an operational SDI will be able to destroy a sufficient portion of an aggressor's attacking forces to deny him confidence in the outcome. Uncertain of achieving his wartime objectives and vulnerable to American reprisals, the likely aggressor will be deterred. Note that the combined effectiveness of the "layered" defenses does not require that all incoming missiles be destroyed—only a sufficiently large number (unspecified) to cause the potential aggressor to lose faith in the benefits of the outcome. As such, the potential aggressor would be much less likely to initiate a nuclear conflict, even in a crisis, if he lacked confidence in his ability to succeed.

The type of deterrence described above (denial of war aims) is different from the type of deterrence (reprisal against military and civilian targets) which previously predominated in American strategic doctrine. Under the type of deterrence envisioned as a result of the SDI, population centers would no longer be held ransom to ensure strategic nuclear war did not occur. Rather, those centers (as well as our own missile forces) are to be defended against nuclear attack. As such, damage to those areas would be reduced in the event of war. This is the same type of deterrence on which American military analysts have focused in promulgating the "flexible response" strategy for defense of Europe. And, it is this war-fighting capability that is so upsetting to NATO Europe. More will be said about this divergence of perspectives later.

Since the concept of deterrence rests on calculations of expected losses and gains, the decision to attack would be affected if the attacker calculated that he could overwhelm the defense sufficiently. This capability is largely a function of the number and type of offensive missiles the attacker could employ. To retard the pendulum from swinging back toward offensive systems (where it is now), some measures limiting the number and/or type of deployed offensive systems must be developed. Arms control measures to ensure the survivability and capability of defensive systems must accompany SDI efforts. SDI backers claim that the results of offensive systems limitation would be twofold: the technical problem of the number of missiles to be defeated could be estimated with greater surety and presumably be reduced from "safe-sided" calculations, thereby requiring fewer resources to solve the entire problem. Additionally, the damage inflicted on America would be less than if Soviet offensive systems were constrained. Proponents for the SDI have also argued that the likelihood of reaching such an agreement is increased given an operational system. They argue that with SDI, the significance of offensive missiles will be lessened. Soviet missiles would be degraded in their ability to inflict damage on the United States, while American missiles would not be forced to evade a Soviet defensive network as formidable as the American's. Knowing this, Soviet arms controllers would have an incentive to bargain.[4] Arms controllers from America would also have a capability with which to bargain—that of offensive missiles. Since American missiles would survive a first strike in greater numbers than if they were undefended, and since those same missiles would have a relatively easier time of evading Soviet defenses, America could better afford to bargain away some of the capacity, especially if the Soviet offensive capacity were to be similarly limited. Since under the SDI concept America is more interested in protecting its homeland than in threatening Soviet cities, it could be expected to concede some of its offensive missile capability to gain Soviet concessions.

In an effort to generate allied (as well as domestic political) support for this ambitious undertaking, the Reagan administration broadened the scope of the research effort and offered to share this emerging technology with its NATO allies. Reacting to European fears of a "decoupling" of the strategic capability of the United States from the defense of Europe, the administration expanded the research concept to include technologies with potential against short range ballistic missiles (SS-20s) and others that are capable of striking the territory of the NATO allies. In so doing, many old wounds of the alliance were made susceptible to reexamination. For better or worse, the SDI is causing a review of our NATO commitment and a discussion of NATO's force posture. From our previous study, certain outcomes for NATO are quite likely as a result of the advent of this new technology.

THE SDI AND NATO

From our examination of the incidence of two previous new weapons technologies on NATO, this author drew the following conclusions:

- The external threat to NATO will be the decisive factor in determining the acceptance of the new weapon technology.
- A new weapon technology is not likely to be accepted by NATO members solely on the basis of its performance characteristics.
- A new weapon technology is likely to become the initiator of divisive debate within NATO. Although military analysts may foresee this new technology as a solution to military deficiencies within the alliance, its actual effect may be quite different.
- The possession of preponderate military power within the alliance has provided the United States with the basis for dominance in setting NATO policy.

Applying these observations to the embryonic SDI technology produces conclusions similar to those derived from the previous examination of the neutron bomb. Regarding the ability of the United States to dominate alliance policy making, that capacity remains limited, precisely for the reasons that have led policy makers to propose a shift in the deterrent strategy inherent in the SDI. The growth of the offensive Soviet strategic capability in both numbers and capability during the 1970s has continued apace in the 1980s. It was a concern for the strategic intentions of the Soviets (as buttressed by the development of capabilities, the doctrinal writings, and the conduct of training exercises by the Soviet military) which led American policy makers to question the Soviet's adherence to the principles of deterrence by Assured Destruction, as supposedly demonstrated by their signing of the SALT I treaties in 1972. Given a force posture which favors adherence to Assured Destruction, America would be at a serious disadvantage against an opponent who was not doctrinally inclined to adhere to the concept of Assured Destruction, and more importantly, had his forces configured to support a war-fighting rather than a war-prevention posture.

In recognition of these obvious disadvantages, American strategic policy makers have been steadily creeping toward a more effective strategic war-fighting capability and a more explicit war-fighting doctrine. However, such efforts have been modest in scale and have met with a considerable outcry from various elements among American strategists. Under SDI, a strategic offensive war-fighting doctrine is eschewed. Rather, proponents of the SDI emphasize its defensive nature and claim it would provide less chance for war to occur initially, and should it occur, to terminate the war on terms more favorable to the United States. The emphasis would not be to punish the Soviets, but to deny them success on the strategic battlefield. As regards NATO, since the SDI is not a prescription for superiority over the Soviets, there would not be a return to American dominance within the policy-making circles of the alliance.

If pursued in a manner similar to that which occurred when the SDI concept was first announced, any American attempt to coerce NATO into public support of this program is likely to test alliance unity. Rather than being seen as a means of reducing tension between the United States and the Soviet Union, and a lever toward reduction in strategic weapons, the SDI has the potential to be the source for divisions within the alliance and between governmental leadership and its people. The reason for this potentially deleterious effect on the alliance is due to the manner in which most Europeans view this technology. Although not all European governments share all of the views listed, they are representative of Europe's position on the issue. As a war-fighting weapon, the SDI technology would be viewed as a device to make war more fightable and, hence, more likely to occur. As such, it would also retard the arms control process. Rather than a means to strengthen deterrence by making it more difficult for the attacker to achieve his goals, deploying the SDI will likely be perceived by NATO Europe as the means to allow war to be confined to Europe and perhaps force a superpower-negotiated termination of hostilities at the expense of Europe's interests. Any of these outcomes is an anathema in European strategic thinking.[5]

War in Europe, regardless of how "limited" it may be in conventional or nuclear terms, is still regarded as catastrophic by Europeans. Termination of hostilities along any lines except the status quo ante is also an unacceptable (at least prior to the war) fate for Europeans. An American attempt to solicit European support for a concept which promises either of these two conditions is in for serious debate within NATO policy-making circles. Obviously, one can be certain that the Soviets will take maximum advantage of any opportunity to foster divisions between members resulting from the debate described above. The point to be remembered here is not who is the winner or loser in the outcome of the debate—all of NATO will be the loser if serious alliance divisions are fostered.

Another perceived drawback of the SDI technology is that it is likely to retard or scuttle the arms control process and spur another round of conventional rearmament. If stability is achieved at the strategic level, Europeans reason the competition will move to the conventional level, an outcome the Europeans are anxious to avoid.[6] Lastly, if the Soviets acquire a workable defensive system (envisioned as part of a "sharing" program with the Soviets, as discussed by the Reagan administration), the utility of all Euromissiles (including both the individual strategic systems of Great Britain and France, and the recently emplaced Pershing II and Ground Launched Cruise Missiles) will be called into question. Since the major states of NATO (except France) have only recently supported the deployment of these missiles at very heavy political costs, they are not anxious to solicit new public support for a system which makes these missiles "impotent and obsolete."

In either case, this debate on the utility of the SDI will likely result in lack of support for the concept by NATO members, especially if the focus of the debate is allowed to remain on the war-fighting characteristics inherent in the concept. The problems of the past, plowed under via compromises which obscured but did not resolve the issue, or subsequent "crises" which shunted one's attention elsewhere, are likely to recur. Concerned about American willingness to confine the war to Europe in hopes of avoiding strategic exchanges, NATO is unlikely to accede willingly to a strategy fraught with unknowns. It is far more likely to remain content with a strategy that has (apparently) worked for nearly forty years, even if that strategy contains inconsistencies. There is no fear so great as fear of the unknown. NATO Europe is likely to conclude that, with so much treasure at risk, it is better to proceed with caution, if at all. Somewhat like Admiral Jellicoe of the British fleet in World War I, the SDI may not have the potential to deter the next war, but it does have the potential to win it. In winning the war, Europe would be the loser.

The foregoing discussion of the reluctance of NATO to accept a new technology that enhances the development of a nuclear war-fighting capability does not mean that NATO Europe will not participate in the development of that technology and ultimately move more toward a nuclear war-fighting posture. Indeed, present indications are that the major states of NATO have already or soon will agree to join in the SDI research effort and it is possible that NATO will ultimately support any American adoption of a deterrent strategy based on the SDI technology.[7] And, if present trends continue, it is probable that NATO Europe will move more in the direction of such a strategy. A major factor in the evolution of NATO Europe's historic position on war-fighting strategies would be the operation of the final conclusion provided by our study: the military force posture of the Soviet Union will determine the degree of NATO acceptance of the new technology. How this evolution might occur and the future of the alliance are subjects for the final portion of this chapter.

Regarding the American adoption of a new deterrent strategy as a result of the SDI-developed technologies, many factors to promote this condition are at work. Some are difficult to measure, but are no less present, and others are familiar to students of the domestic politics of either America or Europe. Five major factors promoting the adoption of this technology by the United States appear to be at work here. First, Americans as a people have always been fascinated by technology and its ability to get the job done. This is as true for products around the home as it is for military hardware. One need only to peer in the average American home to see a wide variety of electronic gadgetry to make life easier or more pleasant. Videotape recorders, personal computers, talking automobiles, and microwave ovens are only a few of the electronic features that are becoming commonplace in America. Within the military, hand-held laser designators, pocket-sized satellite-based navigation systems, and artillery shells that can independently seek and destroy a tank are present in America's military inventory. Rather than merely indicating an affluent society or a defense establishment bent on pursuing exotic gadgets, these devices reflect America's strategic culture and its predisposition for "hi-tech," state-of-the-art hardware. Americans routinely prefer quality to quantity. The lure of a state-of-the-art defensive system has greater appeal for the American psyche than the concept of a "more is better" offensive strategy.

Second, there exists a general belief in America that hardware or technology can solve what are fundamentally political problems. For example, the American proposals regarding the Multi-Lateral Force in the early 1960s, or the bombing of North Vietnam in the late 1960s were attempts by America to solve what were fundamentally political problems by the employment of technology. In both cases, the efforts failed. Americans seem to have an unshakeable belief that technology can provide a shortcut to all kinds of things (reduced tensions between states, for example), or can be a method of avoiding unpleasantness (not invading North Vietnam, but expecting to defeat North Vietnam, for example). Rarely is such an optimistic outcome obtainable.

The third reason for continuing the SDI is one of business. The large sums of research money that are available as a result of the SDI program will prove irresistible for two major reasons: the opportunity to make fundamental advances in scientific knowledge, and the real promise of a secondary application of this technology into non-military areas.

Another reason for continuing with SDI is one of momentum. Once the initial research phase is begun in earnest, almost uncontrollable pressures are formed to continue the research and development momentum. Governmental bureaucracies are formed to foster and regulate the effort, employment opportunities are created in someone's congressional district, and long-term capital investment by business enterprises occurs. Terminating the SDI program after the initial phase in the face of such elements with vested interest in the continuation of the program will be well-nigh impossible.

Lastly, the Soviet Union's insistence on and development of a war-fighting posture, augmented by the development of its own SDI program, will almost certainly be used by the Department of Defense as rationale for a continuation of the program. Individually, any one of these factors would be a powerful argument to continue the program; taken together they will almost certainly be sufficient grounds to cause some form of the SDI program to be continued.

Given the high likelihood of America's pursuit of this technology, there is a possibility, albeit less likely, that NATO Europe will not only pursue the SDI technology, but develop a more self-reliant, war-fighting capability itself. Some of the same factors are at work in Europe as they are in America. The scientific community in Europe is also in need of funds for research purposes, but more than that, Europe's position in the development and application of "hi-tech" research is a distant third to the pace of the United States and Japan, and is steadily worsening.[8] The SDI research proposal, already agreed to by Japan, is Europe's biggest opportunity to date to close the "hi-tech" gap. Business and research interests have strong reasons to favor the program and have pressured the various political leaderships for some share in the opportunity. And, as in the United States, as the business of SDI research gets underway, so will the politics of SDI research. Members of the various European parliaments are no less susceptible to business and popular pressures to continue the research and engage in the development of new job opportunities. If such efforts do result in the development of technology which supports a war-fighting posture, coupled with an American adoption of a more pronounced strategic defense strategy and other political trends in Europe, a very different type of NATO may emerge in the 1990s.

Our assessment of the fate of precision-guided munitions and the neutron bomb in particular and the alliance in general were based on conditions which presently exist. Given the dynamics of the international political system, and domestic political and economic pressures, these conditions may quite likely change in the future, with important implications for our study. Present in these dynamics is the existence on either side of the Atlantic of forces having the potential to change the present structure of NATO, two of which are particularly salient. The political movement toward a united Europe and the potential of the SDI to revive European confidence in its own defense is one scenario that carries good potential for the disintegration of NATO, while the current American attitudes toward the Soviet Union and the NATO allies

and the global perspectives of the United States is another. Either
of these two scenarios alone possesses the very real possibility of
alliance-wrenching impact; occurring simultaneously, their effect
may be synergistic and almost certain to produce a change in the
structure of the alliance. It is not my intention to discuss these
forces in great detail; rather, I will show that conditions within
and without the alliance might well change, thereby affecting the
manner in which NATO is structured and operates, a manner different from what our study has led us to conclude thus far.

A NEW NATO?

Taking these scenarios in reverse order, the Reagan administration, in its early years especially, has exhibited a persistent tendency to engage in strident denunciations of the Soviet Union while
attempting to characterize many of the globe's troubles as Soviet-
inspired. For the United States, the Soviet military buildup is the
greatest source of world tensions and the relative decline in American military power allows that tension to grow. This anti-Soviet
stance set off a determined program to "re-arm" the American
military in an attempt to demonstrate both leadership to its allies
and resolve to the Soviets. But this program of military expansion
came at a time when the administration was also determined to
reduce the scope and scale of most government entitlement programs and the burden of taxes. The hoped-for economic upturn
as a result of these budgetary policies is apparent, but soaring budget deficits and a more intractable Congress make the likelihood
of cuts in planned military spending most probable.[9]
Within the administration and certain elements of Congress, there
exists an almost chronic complaint that the Europeans are not providing their fair share of defense support to NATO, nor are they
willing to support actively many American foreign policy initiatives, some of which are related to NATO, some not. Many
American attempts to generate full support for its policies have
been rebuffed, occasionally not very politely. While these have
been persistent American charges over the years, it is significant
that in the present case the terms "Vicheyite," "neutralist," and
"pacifist" have been used to describe European attitudes.[10] While

it is possible that these views toward NATO Europe are more deeply felt within this particular administration, the declining military manpower pool and the widespread American opposition to resumption of the draft are not.[11] It is quite likely that the culmination of these factors will draw America away from NATO as the main defense effort and toward another area, most likely the Persian/Arabian Gulf. The extensive energy resources there, the vulnerability of those energy lifelines to armed attack, and lack of sufficient forces not already committed to a NATO contingency to provide anything more than a nominal show of force in that area point toward a reordering of American defense priorities. When combined with the above-mentioned problems of dissatisfaction with the defense efforts of Europe, high American military spending on the SDI project in an era of domestic budget cutbacks, and a declining manpower pool for the military, the likelihood of some amount of American withdrawal of some forces directly related to NATO appears real.

If the possibility of a reallocation of American forces from NATO exists because of domestic factors within the United States and concern over European appreciation of the Soviet threat, that action may coincide with political changes in Europe—the second possible scenario mentioned above.

The implications of an American adoption of a more defensive strategic doctrine as a result of the technologies inherent in the SDI are significant for Europe. The technologies that produce the possibility of a strategic defense of the American homeland can also produce a defense of Europe. If, as part of the SDI research effort, European companies were to develop technologies suitable for a defense against short-range missiles, that capability might coincide with the political unification of Europe. If, as Henry Kissinger has noted, the dependence of Europe on the United States for its security is "not natural," it seems reasonable to believe that this unnatural state would be overturned at some time. The period of political unification would be that time. The trend toward this unification is clear, if slow. With Turkey's acceptance, all European members of NATO except Norway will be members of the European Economic Community. Eurodollars are in increasingly common usage. A European Parliament has been elected and soon a European party system will be established. A judicial court for Europe now exists in the Netherlands. Again, progress toward unity has been slow, but steady. A final component of that unity which would lead toward true independence would be physical security brought about by a European military force. Such a Europe could not be dependent on the United States as the final guarantor of its survival. A nuclear-armed Europe with Great Britain and France (and some form of a nuclear-occupied but not nuclear-armed Germany) supplying the strategic offensive capability which also depended upon a defensive capability developed through SDI-related research is a real possibility before the millennium. A precondition of such an arrangement would be the absolute certainty of West Germany's participation and its total immersion within such an arrangement. An armed West Germany outside the context of some form of European military alliance is not politically acceptable to the remainder of Western Europe, or to the Germans themselves. Whatever the form of such a consortium, it is probable that such a political entity would be more neutral than pro-American, spelling the end of NATO.

The prospect of a neutral, armed Europe without the NATO of today has some significant drawbacks, but is not too frightful for Americans to contemplate. The major drawback is a further decrease of the American leverage with NATO states. More than any other benefit, the dependence of NATO Europe on the United States for its survival has provided the United States with a great deal of political leverage over Europe during the past decades, but that leverage is now quite diminished. If the original purpose of NATO was to provide the means to prevent the Soviets from occupying Western Europe, and a united, armed but neutral Europe without NATO accomplishes the same goal, then the United States has only lost that which it did not have much of anyway. Too often, military analysts tend to think of NATO as a foreign policy goal, to be pursued as an end unto itself, rather than a policy instrument to be used or modified as required in response to changing circumstances. If NATO has outlived its usefulness, or will be more effective if altered, then so be it. The benefits of a reduced (lack of) American presence in Europe are that the forces could be used elsewhere, as previously discussed. Calling these defense savings "benefits" may just be a perverse form of "sour grapes" anyway—an attempt to put a good face on the inevitable outcome.

U.S. RELATIONS WITH NATO

Regardless of whether one would like to see America rid of the major responsibility for Europe's defense within the strictures of NATO, America should continue to seek to improve its relations with NATO and enhance alliance cohesion in general. Our study of new weapons technology has suggested some techniques which might accomplish those ends. It should be noted that whether these techniques would enhance the cohesion of NATO, or serve to make NATO Europe more independent of the United States and thus cause NATO's disintegration is problematical. That occurrence is also largely irrelevant if it accomplishes the same goal (at an acceptable cost) of retarding a Soviet advance or projection of political influence into Western Europe. Additionally, if this author has been critical of the manner in which previous forms of new technology have been introduced into the alliance, it is incumbent upon him to prescribe some alternatives to the present manner in which policies are being pursued.

Perhaps the most fundamental guideline for American defense officials charged with relations with NATO would be to refrain from making the acceptance of a new weapon technology a litmus test of support for the alliance. Loud, public rhetoric about the constancy of one's allies is not likely to cause them to adopt one's preferred course of action, and may possibly prove counterproductive. As this study on new weapon technologies has noted, there is a variety of reasons why states adopt particular courses of action. Some of those reasons are rooted in the international environment, while others have more to do with a state's "strategic culture," with other domestic reasons, or some mix of these. Proclaiming publicly (via leaks to the media or statements on the agenda of conferences) that state X is not providing its fair share (whatever *that* is supposed to mean) will likely result in state X supplying large amounts of data to demonstrate that, indeed, it *is* making a proportional contribution to the alliance in a variety of ways.

Such debate, particularly if carried by the media, will not likely resolve the problem and may only generate ill feelings since no state enjoys being coerced into any policy and few states would ever admit to being coerced. Rather, legitimate attempts to persuade allies about the wisdom of particular policies should be done in private, and should focus on furthering the goals of the alliance rather than on criticisms of members who are not persuaded. American officials should not attempt to identify the reason for non-support of the proposed policy ("pacifist" tendencies, "Vicheyite," etc.), but instead should concentrate their arguments on the benefits of the policy or technology. If the new technology is accused by Europeans of undercutting the American strategic guarantee, rather than denying that charge, American officials would do better by explaining how the new technology would enhance the guarantee (presuming that it does).

American officials would do well also to cite the non-military benefits of the new technology. Usually some degree of political, economic, or social benefit accrues to the user and developer of the new technology. Perhaps more jobs would be created in fielding the equipment associated with the new technology; perhaps military manpower savings would result with its adoption; or perhaps more political power will devolve to the less powerful members of the alliance. These are the sorts of benefits that may be emphasized in lieu of the military benefits. Since it is the military war-fighting potential that Europeans have found so bothersome in the past about new technologies, it would make more sense to downplay those aspects of the new technology, especially in public discussions. Because public support of a new technology is critical, especially in Europe with its well-developed left-oriented parties and somewhat fragile governing coalitions, particular care must be taken to avoid arousing public sensibilities. President Reagan's offhand comment about confining a nuclear war to Europe is a case in point. When asked about such a possibility, the president responded that he "guessed" it could. Different perspectives on the same issue must be fully understood and appreciated by American policy officials. Antagonizing NATO Europe with such comments by an American president is inexcusable and compounds the difficulty in maintaining positive alliance relationships.

In reviewing the need for the new technology, one should explicitly link the technology to the existence of a particular threat—the more proximate the threat, the more effective the argument. Additionally, the ineffectiveness of alternative weapons and technologies should be explained. The costs of not pursuing the technology should also be part of the review.

To the degree possible, the states of NATO Europe should be made to appear to have the lead in the discussions regarding the new technology. The United States should downplay its role in the development of the technology and attempt to involve Europe to the maximum extent in the economic benefits surrounding its development.

Lastly, every effort must be made to link the new technology to progress in arms control and a slowing of the arms races—both the strategic race between the superpowers, and the conventional arms buildup on the continent. While it may seem contradictory to pursue new weapons as a means of limiting them, it may be that some new technologies will render classes of weapons obsolete (thereby making reductions in them easier to negotiate) or allow the development of new strategies which will reduce reliance on certain classes of weapons. Alternatively some new technologies may make arms verification processes easier or less provocative, thereby aiding the arms control process.

The techniques described above may smack of Madison Avenue salesmanship (to a degree they are) and therefore imply that NATO can be deceived—that America can foist onto Europe something that is deleterious to its interests. That is not at all the intention of this author. Throughout this study, it has been clear that in too many instances, America has been insensitive to the perspectives, political cultures, and limitations of its NATO allies. With an increased degree of sophistication and tact, many of the effects of these problems could have been minimized. NATO Europe is fully capable of assessing its own various needs. Given time, it usually adopts a view supportive of U.S. policy. It might adopt that view more quickly if the United States were a bit better at diplomacy and alliance management.

Regardless of one's thoughts on the future direction of NATO, it seems clear that weapon technology by itself cannot change what are essentially the political problems of NATO. To place reliance on new weapon technologies to enhance alliance cohesion and efficacy is a misdirected strategy. If NATO's past is instructive, previous new technologies have produced consequences unforeseen by their proponents quite apart from those which would be revealed by an examination of only their military characteristics. This study has attempted to reveal those factors which are most critical to the future of a technology and to NATO, and to suggest ways of minimizing adverse consequences. To this end, it is hoped that some past sins can be avoided. Or, at least one will have a better grasp on the nature of the sins he commits in the future.

NOTES

1. *Weekly Compilation of Presidential Documents.* Vol. 19, No. 12, 28 March 1983, pp. 442–48.

2. The $26 billion has been requested by the administration for FY86–90.

3. U.S. Congress, Office of Technology Assessment. *Ballistic Missile Defense Technologies*, (Washington, DC: U.S. Government Printing Office, 1985).

4. Opponents of the SDI program argue (correctly) that the Soviet Union is not likely to throw up its hands in despair (offer reductions in its missile strength) when faced with an American advantage. Historically, the Soviet response has been to redress the imbalance. See Harold Brown, "The Strategic Defense Initiative: Defensive Systems and the Strategic Debate," *Survival* 27 (March/April 1985): 55.

5. Helmut Kohl, speech to the CDU National Convention, Essen, FRG, 20 March 1985, as cited in Victor S. Gray, "Alliance Cohesion in the Era of SDI," unpublished paper, p. 23.

6. Helmut Kohl, address to *Wehrkunde*, Munich FRG, 9 February 1985, as cited in Gray, "Alliance Cohesion," p. 31; William J. Broad, "Allies in Europe Are Apprehensive About Benefits of 'Star Wars' Plan," *New York Times*, 13 May 1985, p. 1.

7. As of this writing, Great Britain has formally agreed to participate, West Germany has agreed to allow private firms to participate, France is leaning in that direction, and Italy is interested in the project, but is undecided on the manner and extent of its participation. Of the smaller

states of NATO, the Netherlands, Spain, and Belgium have indicated a willingness to participate also.

8. Judith Miller, "Allies in West Lend Support to 'Star Wars,'" *New York Times* 30 December 1985, p. 1.

9. Many critics of the Reagan administration feel that the economic upturn is due to Keynesian economics—spending by the government, especially on the military's budget—rather than the supply side economics touted by the Regan administration in its early years.

10. Leslie H. Gelb, "NATO is Facing a Paralysis of Will, Experts Contend," *New York Times*, 12 July 1981, p. 1.

11. Recent estimates of the proportion of qualified and available (mentally and physically qualified, not college-bound) males required annually for military service range from 50 to 77 percent, depending on the total end strength of the services. There is great likelihood that the end strength of the services will decline, however, over the next several years. *See* Martin Binkin, *Military Technology and Defense Manpower* (Washington, D.C.: The Brookings Institution, 1986), pp. 80–82.

Appendix 1
Defense Spending as a Percentage of Gross National Product by Selected NATO States

State	Fiscal Year														
	1953	1955	1957	1959	1961	1963	1965	1967	1969	1971	1973	1975	1977	1979	1981
Great Britain	10.0	8.2	7.2	6.6	6.3	6.2	6.0	5.8	5.1	5.1	4.8	4.5	4.8	4.8	5.4
West Germany	4.2	4.1	4.1	4.4	4.0	5.2	4.3	4.3	3.6	3.4	3.5	3.6	3.4	3.3	4.3
France	9.1	6.4	7.3	6.6	6.2	5.6	5.2	5.0	4.4	3.9	3.8	3.8	3.9	3.9	4.1
Belgium	4.8	3.8	3.6	3.5	3.3	3.4	3.2	3.1	2.9	2.8	2.8	3.1	3.2	3.3	3.3
Italy	3.8	3.7	3.5	3.3	3.1	3.3	3.3	3.1	2.7	3.0	2.9	2.5	2.4	2.4	2.5
Netherlands	5.6	5.7	5.2	4.0	4.5	4.4	3.9	3.9	3.6	3.5	3.2	3.5	3.4	3.4	3.4
Turkey	4.9	5.1	4.1	4.5	5.0	4.6	4.8	4.4	4.4	4.5	4.3	6.0	6.0	4.9	4.5
Norway	5.1	3.9	3.6	3.6	3.3	3.5	3.7	3.4	3.6	3.4	3.1	3.2	3.1	3.1	3.3
United States	13.4	10.0	9.9	9.4	9.1	8.8	7.5	9.4	8.6	6.9	6.7	6.0	5.4	5.2	6.1

SOURCE: Stockholm International Peace Research Institute, World Armaments and Disarmament, SIPRI Yearbook 1981 (London: Taylor and Francis, Ltd., 1981), p. 166; International Institute for Strategic Studies, The Military Balance (London: International Institute for Strategic Studies, 1983), p. 124; and NATO Information Service, NATO: Facts and Figures (Brussels: NATO Information Service, 1976), pp. 294-95.

NOTE: All figures for defense spending are in accordance with the NATO (not national) definition.

Appendix 2

Military Personnel Strength of Selected NATO States (thousands of persons)

State	Calendar Year														
	1953	1955	1957	1959	1961	1963	1965	1967	1969	1971	1973	1975	1977	1979	1981
Great Britain	865	802	702	565	520	430	424	417	383	365	352	340	330	323	344
West Germany				249	270	403	441	452	465	467	475	495	489	495	495
France				770	781	632	510	500	503	502	504	503	502	509	505
Belgium				120	110	110	107	102	102	97	90	87	86	87	89
Italy				400	466	420	390	416	420	414	427	421	330	365	366
Netherlands				130	142	141	135	130	124	117	112	113	110	115	103
Turkey				500	500	452	442	480	483	509	455	453	456	566	569
Norway				40	37	36	32	35	38	36	35	35	39	39	37
United States	3555	2935	2796	2435	2606	2700	2660	3400	3454	2699	2253	2130	2088	2022	2049

SOURCE: International Institute for Strategic Studies, The Military Balance (London: International Institute for Strategic Studies), 1959, pp. 8-11; 1961, pp. 14-21; 1963, p. 33; 1965, pp. 15-27; 1967, 1969, pp. 17-31; 1969, p. 59; 1979, pp. 12, 96; 1982, p. 112; Lawrence Freeman, "Britain's Defense Policy," in Defense Politics of the Atlantic Alliance, ed. Edwin H. Fedder, (New York: Praeger Publishers, 1981), p. 53; and U.S. Department of Commerce, Statistical Abstract of the United States, 1954, 1956, 1958.

Appendix 3
Selected Air-to-Surface PGMs

Designation	Developed by	Range (km)	Weight of Device (lb.)a	Guidance	Comments
AS.30	France	12	1,150	Radio Command, some automatic features	Can be used against hard points and ships
AS.30 Laser	France	12	1,150	Laser homing	Replaces AS.20
AM.39 Exocet	France	70	1,450	Radar homing	Air, ship and shore-launched versions
AS.37 Martel	France/ Britain	30–60	1,170	Passive radio frequency	For attacks on radar
AJ.168 Martel	Britain/ France	30–60	1,215	TV link + radio command	Can be steered by land-marks till target comes
Maverick AGM-65	USA	b	460	TV tracker	Tracks automatically after lock-on
Rockeye KMU-420	USA	c	500	Laser homing	Primarily for antitank
Modular-Guided Glide bomb	USA	80(?)	2,000	TV or other radio command	Evolving program related to MK-84 HOBOS

Designation	Developed by	Range (km)	Weight of Round (1b.)	Guidance	Comments
Shrike AGM-45A	USA	12-16	390	Passive radio frequency seeker	Used against ground radars
Standard ARM AGM-78A/B/C/D	USA	>25	1,795	Passive radio frequency seeker	Used against ground radars
AGM-88A Harm	USA	20	800	Antiradiation, radar seeker	Replaces Shrike and standard ARM
MK-82-LGB KMU-388B	USA	c	500	Laser homing seeking	Steerable bomb
Mk-82-LGB KMU-351B	USA	c	2,000	Laser homing	Steerable bomb
MK-84-HOBOS KMU-353A/B	USA	c	2,000	TV homing	Steerable bomb
MK-84-IR Paveway KMU-359B	USA	c	2,000	Laser homing	Steerable bomb
Bulldog AGM-83A	USA	10	598	Laser homing	Derived from older Bullpup versions

Designation	Developed by	Range (km)	Weight of Round (lb.)	Guidance	Comments
AGM-84A Harpoon	USA	90	1,500	Radar homing	Air and sea-launched versions
Condor AGM-53A	USA	110	2,110	Electro-optical/TV homing or command	Remotely piloted
Walleye I	USA	c	1,100	Electro-optical/TV homing or command	Carried by F-4, A-7, etc.
Walleye II	USA	c	2,330	Electro-optical/TV homing or command	Used against large, semi-hard targets, e.g., bridges, ships

SOURCE: Extracted from James Digby, "Precison-Guided Weapons," _Adelphi Papers_, No. 118 (London: International Institute for Strategic Studies, 1975), p. 14; _Jane's Weapons Systems_, 1981-1982.

a. In this table only, to agree with common American and British usage, weights are given in pounds. Bomb weights are nominal and actual weights may be 10 percent more or less.

b. Aerodynamic range has been given as 22km, but practical range for guided launch has not been revealed.

c. Free fall.

Designation	Developed by	Minimum/Maximum Range (meters)	Weight of Round (kg)	Guidance	Comments
ENTAC	France	400/3000	12.0	Manual command	Production complete, 13,000 produced
SS-11/AS-11	France	350/3000	29.9	Manual Command	Antisubmarine version for helicopters; 174,000 produced
SS-12/AS-12	France	800/6000	76.0	Semiautomatic	Antisubmarine version for helicopters. 6,000 max. range helicopter, 8,000 max. from aircraft
HOT	France/ Germany	75/4000	23.5	Semiautomatic command	May be used in light helicopter
Cobra 2000	Germany	400/2000	10.3	Manual command	Production has ceased
Mamba	Germany	300/2000	11.2	Optical tracked, wire-guided	Ground fired
Milan	France/ Germany	25/2000	6.7	Semiautomatic command	Two-man crew
Swingfire	Britain	150/4000	34.0	Manual command plus aids	Operator can be offset 100 m, vehicle in defilade

Designation	Developed by	Minimum/Maximum Range (meters)	Weight of Round (kg)	Guidance	Comments
TOW BGM-71A	USA	65/3750	19.0	Semiautomatic command, wire-guided	Many carriers, but M-113 APC and AH1-S Cobra predominate in US Army
Dragon M-47	USA	?/1000	6.3	Semiautomatic command	Man-portable, wire guided
Snapper AT-1	USSR	500/2300	22.0	Manual command	Used in several Pact armies. Mounts on BRDM armored reconnaissance vehicle
Swatter AT-2	USSR	500/3500	29.4	Manual command, possible infrared terminal guidance	Mounts on APC and BRDM
Sagger AT-3	USSR	500/3000	11.0	Manual command, wire-guided	Mounts on APC and BRDM
Spigot AT-4	USSR	2000 (est.)	12.0 (est)	Optical tracked, wire-guided	Man-portable

SOURCE: Extracted from James Digby, "Precision-Guided Munitions," Adelphi Papers, No. 118 (London: International Institute for Strategic Studies, 1975,), p. 15, and Jane's Weapon Systems, 1981-1982.

Appendix 5
Selected Surface-to-Air PGMs

Designation	Developed by	Altitude Limits (meters)	Guidance	Comments
Crotale	France	50/3000	Multi-Mode	Mounts on tracked or wheeled carrier
Roland II	France/Germany	50/3000	Optical and radar	Mounts on tracked vehicle; tentatively adopted by the US Army in 1975; dropped from inventory 1982
Rapier	Britain	6000	Optical or with Blindfire radar	Tracked or towed versions
Blowpipe	Britain	(?)	Optical plus radio command	Shoulder-fired
Redeye	USA	Probably 3000	Optical aiming, infrared homing	Shoulder-fired
Stinger FIM-92A	USA	Probably 3000	Optical aiming, infrared homing	Shoulder-fired; in development to replace Redeye
SA-6 Gainful	USSR	About 18,000	Radar or optical	Mounted in threes on a tracked carrier
SA-7 Grail	USSR	50/1500	Optical aiming, infrared homing	Shoulder-fired or in batteries on tracks

SOURCE: Extracted from James Digby, "Precision-Guided Weapons," Adelphi Papers, No. 118 (London: International Institute for Strategic Studies, 1975), p. 16, and Jane's Weapon Systems, 1981–1982.

Selected Bibliography

Aron, Raymond. *The Great Debate*. Garden City, NY: Doubleday and Co., Inc., 1965.

Barnett, Frank R. Forward to "Nuclear Weapons and the Atlantic Alliance," *Strategy Papers*, No. 18. New York: National Strategy Information Center, 1973.

Beaufre, Andre. *NATO and Europe*. Translated by Joseph Green. New York: Vintage Books, 1966.

Brodie, Bernard. *Strategy in the Missile Age*. Princeton: Princeton University Press, 1959.

———. *War and Politics*. New York: Macmillan Co., 1973.

Brown, Seyom. *The Faces of Power: Constancy and Change in U.S. Foreign Policy from Truman to Johnson*. New York: Columbia University Press, 1969.

———. New Forces in World Politics. Washington, DC: The Brookings Institution, 1974.

Bundy, McGeorge; Kennan, George; McNamara, Robert S.; and Smith, Gerard. "Nuclear Weapons and the Atlantic Alliance." *Foreign Affairs* 60 (Spring 1982): 753–68.

Burt, Richard A. "The Debate on the New Weapons Technology." *Adelphi Papers*, No. 126. London: International Institute for Strategic Studies, Summer 1976.

Canby, Steven. "The Alliance and Europe: Part IV, Military Doctrine and Technology." *Adelphi Papers*, No. 109. London: International Institute for Strategic Studies, Winter 1974–75.

Congressional Research Service. "Enhanced Radiation Weapons: The

'Neutron Bomb.' " Issue Brief IB78085. Washington, DC: Library of Congress, 1979.

Daumas, Maurice, ed. *A History of Technology and Invention*. New York: Crown Publications, 1969.

Digby, James. "Precision-Guided Weapons." *Adelphi Papers*, No. 118. London: International Institute for Strategic Studies, 1975.

Enthoven, Alain C., and Smith, K. Wayne. *How Much Is Enough?* New York: Harper and Row, 1971; Harper Colophon, 1972.

Fedder, Edwin H. *NATO: The Dynamics of Alliance in the Post-War World*. New York: Dodd, Mead and Co., 1973.

Fuller, J. F. C. *Armament and History*. New York: Charles Scribner's Sons, 1945.

Gaddis, John Lewis. "Containment: A Reassessment." *Foreign Affairs* 55 (July 1977): 873–87.

———. *Strategies of Containment*. New York: Oxford University Press, 1982.

———. *The United States and the Origins of the Cold War, 1941–1947*. New York: Columbia University Press, 1972.

Gallois, Pierre M. "U.S. Strategy and the Defense of Europe." *Orbis* 7 (Summer 1963): 226–49.

Gardner, Richard N. *Sterling Dollar Diplomacy: The Origins and Prospects of Our International Economic Order*. Exp. ed. New York: McGraw-Hill, 1969.

Gelb, Leslie H. "NATO is Facing Paralysis of Will, Experts Contend," *New York Times*, 12 July 1981, p. 1.

George, Alexander L., and Smoke, Richard. *Deterrence in American Foreign Policy: Theory and Practice*. New York: Columbia University Press, 1974.

Hart, B. H. Liddell. *Deterrent or Defense*. New York: Praeger Publishers, 1960.

Huntington, Samuel P. *The Common Defense*. New York: Columbia University Press, 1961.

Inglehart, Ronald. *The Silent Revolution*. Princeton: Princeton University Press, 1977.

Kegley, Charles W., and Wittkopf, Eugene R. *American Foreign Policy: Pattern and Process*. New York: St. Martin's Press, 1982.

Kennan, George F. [Mr.X]. "The Sources of Soviet Conduct." *Foreign Affairs* 25 (July 1947): 566–82.

Kissinger, Henry A. "NATO: The Next Thirty Years." *Survival* 21 (November/December 1979): 264–68.

———. *Nuclear Weapons and Foreign Policy*. New York: Harper Brothers, 1957.

————. *White House Years.* Boston: Little, Brown and Co., 1979.

Knorr, Klaus. "The Atlantic Alliance: A Reappraisal." *Headline Series,* No. 221. New York: Foreign Policy Association, 1974.

Lineberry, William P. *The U.S. in World Affairs 1970.* New York: Simon and Schuster, 1972.

Liska, George. *Nations in Alliance: The Limits of Interdependence.* Baltimore: Johns Hopkins University Press, 1962.

Meyers, Kenneth A., ed. *NATO: The Next Thirty Years.* Boulder, CO: Westview Press, 1980.

Montross, Lynn. *War Through the Ages.* 3rd ed. New York: Harper and Row, 1960.

NATO Information Service. *NATO—Facts About the North Atlantic Organization.* Paris: NATO Information Service, 1962.

Osgood, Robert E. *NATO: The Entangling Alliance.* Chicago: University of Chicago Press, 1962.

Pierre, Andrew J. "Can Europe's Security Be 'Decoupled' from America's?" *Foreign Affairs* 51 (July 1973): 761–77.

Quester, George H. *Nuclear Diplomacy.* New York: The Dunellen Publishing Co., Inc., 1970.

————. *Offense and Defense in the International System.* New York: John Wiley and Sons, 1977.

Rosenberg, David A. "American Atomic Strategy and the Hydrogen Bomb Decision." *Journal of American History* 66 (June 1979): 64–69.

————. "A Smoking, Radiating Ruin at the End of Two Hours: Documents on American Plans for Nuclear War with the Soviet Union, 1954–1955." *International Security* 6 (Winter 1981/82): 3–71.

Schelling, Thomas C. *The Strategy of Conflict.* Cambridge: Harvard University Press, 1960.

Schilling, Warner R.; Hammond, Paul Y.; and Snyder, Glenn H. *Strategy, Politics, and Defense Budgets.* New York: Columbia University Press, 1962.

Schmidt, Helmut. *Defense or Retaliation: A German View.* New York: Praeger Publishers, 1962.

Sloan, Stanley R. "Crisis in NATO: A Problem in Leadership?" *NATO Review* 30 (August 1980): 13–19.

Snyder, Glenn H. *Deterrence and Defense.* Princeton: Princeton University Press, 1961.

Spanier, John W. *American Foreign Policy Since World War II.* 9th ed. New York: Holt, Rinehart and Winston, 1983.

Spero, Joan Edelman. *The Politics of International Economic Relations.* New York: St. Martin's Press, Inc., 1977.

Stanley, Timothy W. *NATO in Transition: The Future of the Atlantic Alliance.* New York: Praeger Publishers, 1965.

Stebbins, Richard P. *The U.S. in World Affairs 1967.* New York: Simon and Schuster, 1968.

Stoessinger, John. *Henry Kissinger: The Anguish of Power.* New York: W. W. Norton and Co., 1976.

U.S. Department of Defense. *The Theater Nuclear Force Posture in Europe,* James R. Schlesinger, A Report to the U.S. Congress in Compliance with Public Law 93-365. Washington, DC: U.S. Government Printing Office, 1975.

U.S. Department of State. *American Foreign Policy 1950–1955.* Basic Documents Pubn. 6446 (1957).

Van Cleave, William R., and Cohen, S. T. *Tactical Nuclear Weapons: An Examination of the Issues.* New York: Crane, Russak and Company, Inc., 1978.

Wolfers, Arnold., ed. *Alliance Policy in the Cold War.* Baltimore: Johns Hopkins University Press, 1959.

Index

About the Author

ROBERT KROMER, a retired Lieutenant Colonel with operational assignments in NATO, received his Ph.D. in International Relations from Duke University. He is the co-author, with Amos A. Jordan, William J. Taylor, and Associates, of *American National Security: Policy and Process*.